THE COMPLETE GUIDE TO

Making Cheese, Butter, and Yogurt At Home

Everything You Need to Know Explained Simply

By Richard Helweg

THE COMPLETE GUIDE TO MAKING CHEESE, BUTTER, AND YOGURT AT HOME: EVERYTHING YOU NEED TO KNOW EXPLAINED SIMPLY

Library of Congress Cataloging-in-Publication Data

Helweg, Richard, 1956-
  The complete guide to making cheese, butter, and yogurt at home : everything you need to know explained simply / by Richard Helweg.
      p. cm.
  Includes bibliographical references and index.
  ISBN-13: 978-1-60138-355-6 (alk. paper)
  ISBN-10: 1-60138-355-X (alk. paper)
  1. Cheese. 2. Cheese--Varieties. 3. Cookery (Cheese) I. Title.
  SF271.H45 2010   *641.67 H 3/8/13*
  637.3--dc22   *Hel*
                          2009054423

Printed in the United States

PROJECT MANAGER: Amy Moczynski • amoczynski@atlantic-pub.com
ASSISTANT EDITOR: Angela Pham • apham@atlantic-pub.com
PEER REVIEWER: Marilee Griffin • mgriffin@atlantic-pub.com
INTERIOR DESIGN: Samantha Martin • smartin@atlantic-pub.com
FRONT & BACK COVER DESIGN: Jackie Miller • millerjackiej@gmail.com

Printed on Recycled Paper

A few years back we lost our beloved pet dog Bear, who was not only our best and dearest friend but also the "Vice President of Sunshine" here at Atlantic Publishing. He did not receive a salary but worked tirelessly 24 hours a day to please his parents.

Bear was a rescue dog who turned around and showered myself, my wife, Sherri, his grandparents Jean, Bob, and Nancy, and every person and animal he met (well, maybe not rabbits) with friendship and love. He made a lot of people smile every day.

We wanted you to know a portion of the profits of this book will be donated in Bear's memory to local animal shelters, parks, conservation organizations, and other individuals and nonprofit organizations in need of assistance.

– Douglas & Sherri Brown

PS: We have since adopted two more rescue dogs: first Scout, and the following year, Ginger. They were both mixed golden retrievers who needed a home.

Want to help animals and the world? Here are a dozen easy suggestions you and your family can implement today:

- *Adopt and rescue a pet from a local shelter.*
- *Support local and no-kill animal shelters.*
- *Plant a tree to honor someone you love.*
- *Be a developer — put up some birdhouses.*
- *Buy live, potted Christmas trees and replant them.*
- *Make sure you spend time with your animals each day.*
- *Save natural resources by recycling and buying recycled products.*
- *Drink tap water, or filter your own water at home.*
- *Whenever possible, limit your use of or do not use pesticides.*
- *If you eat seafood, make sustainable choices.*
- *Support your local farmers markets.*
- *Get outside. Visit a park, volunteer, walk your dog, or ride your bike.*

Five years ago, Atlantic Publishing signed the Green Press Initiative. These guidelines promote environmentally friendly practices, such as using recycled stock and vegetable-based inks, avoiding waste, choosing energy-efficient resources, and promoting a no-pulping policy. We now use 100-percent recycled stock on all our books. The results: in one year, switching to post-consumer recycled stock saved 24 mature trees, 5,000 gallons of water, the equivalent of the total energy used for one home in a year, and the equivalent of the greenhouse gases from one car driven for a year.

DEDICATION

This book is for Karen, Aedan, and Rory for sharing their refrigerator with all of my cheese, butter, and yogurt. Also, I dedicate this book to all of my friends and neighbors for taking in copious amounts of dairy products.

TABLE OF CONTENTS

PART TWO: Butter   43

Chapter 3: Spreading the Word on Butter   45

Chapter 4: How to Make Butter   49

Chapter 5: Beyond Basic Butter   57

Chapter 11: Making Soft Cheeses   127

Chapter 12: Making Italian Cheese   167

Chapter 16: Great Recipes with Cheese, Butter, and Yogurt   261

Conclusion   273

Resources   275

Glossary   277

Bibliography   281

Biography   283

Index   285

INTRODUCTION

"This cheese is delicious! Where did you get it?" Imagine being able to answer, "I made it." People who love to prepare food take great pleasure in sharing what they have made with others. This book will help you add some incredible new dishes to your repertoire.

Chances are if you are reading this book, you like to work and play in the kitchen. Whether you enjoy baking breads, preparing desserts, or creating gourmet dishes, making cheese, butter, and yogurt can complement just about any of your favorite foods.

If you enjoy preparing food, you know how satisfying it can be to cut into a freshly baked loaf of bread or open a bottle of homemade wine. Making your own cheese, butter, and yogurt delivers the same wonderful satisfaction.

The mission of this book is to be a complete guide to making cheese, butter, and yogurt at home. It is everything you need to know about making cheese, butter, and yogurt — explained simply.

To explain the process of preparing these creamery items in your home, it is best to start with the simple process of making butter, and that is how this book will begin. This book will take you from the surprising simplicity of butter to the complexity of making your own aged bacteria- and mold-ripened cheeses.

Making creamery items is a culinary skill the whole family can enjoy. Making butter, yogurt, and cheese can be a fun and educational experience for kids as well as adults. The recipes for butter and easy Mozzarella are great for chefs of all ages and skill levels. Get the kids involved as you learn about how cream and milk change with shaking and heating. You will be fascinated by understanding how milk separates into curds and whey. (The curd is the solid mass that results from the heating and ripening of milk, and whey is the liquid that separates from the solids in the milk.) This curd can be cut, stretched, strained, drained, broiled, and baked, while the whey can be used to make cheese, bake bread, soften pizza crust, and much more. There is no limit as to what can be done with a gallon of milk.

In this book, you will learn about all of the ingredients and utensils you will need to make a wide range of homemade creamery items. You will learn how to clean and care for your equipment, making sure everything remains sanitary so your dairy products are always safe to eat. You will learn many of the basic techniques necessary to transform simple milk and cream into butter, yogurt, and many kinds of cheeses. There are many recipes for making butter, yogurt, and cheese, as well as recipes for foods that can be prepared with butter, yogurt, cheese, and the by-products of these items.

Though making butter, yogurt, and cheese can be rewarding in many ways, be careful about going into this as a money-saving proposition. For the most part, you are not going to save any money making your own butter and cheese unless you have a good source of inexpensive milk and cream. However, you can save money when making your own yogurt because once you have a good yogurt starter going, the only cost is the quart of milk you will use, which is less expensive than a quart of store-bought yogurt.

All things considered, the biggest advantages to making your own cheese, butter, and yogurt are their taste and the fact you know exactly what went into the production of each and every item. Once you have a bowl of fresh, homemade yogurt with fresh cherries or any of your favorite fruit, you may never go back to store-bought yogurt. The same is true of homemade butter, buttermilk, cream cheese, or any of the products described in this book.

This book is divided into four parts to easily explore step-by-step the processes of making wonderful creamery products in your home kitchen. The book is designed to get you established with the equipment and ingredients you will need and then to take you from the easiest process through the more complex and time-consuming process of advanced cheese making.

The first part of the book looks at your kitchen and describes the equipment you will need to get started. The first part will also discuss some of the ingredients basic to making cheese, butter, and yogurt and where you can procure some of the harder-to-find items, such as real buttermilk, raw milk (farm-fresh, unprocessed milk), and cheese starters.

The second part looks at all things butter. Here, we will take a fun look at the history of butter and will then learn a variety of ways you can make and store butter in your kitchen. This part will also examine butter variations and by-products. Part Two will conclude with recipes using butter and related products, such as a butter piecrust, buttermilk pancakes, and buttermilk quark. Many Americans are not familiar with quark, but as you will learn in this book, quark is a delicious cream cheese-like substance that is easy to make — and quite addictive.

Part Three explores yogurt and begins with a history of this simple yet complex food. This section will describe various methods of making and storing yogurt in your kitchen as well as describing ways to make several products related to yogurt, such as yogurt cheese and frozen yogurt. Like Part Two, Part Three will conclude with recipes you can make that use yogurt or products related to yogurt. Recipes from this section include yogurt biscuits, smoothies, and a wonderful yogurt dip called tzatziki.

In Part Four of this book, we will turn to cheese and begin by taking a look at the long history of cheese. We will continue by examining some of the basic processes you will need to know that are common to most cheese-making methods. We will review some of the cheese-specific ingredients and equipment that were not explored in chapters 1 and 2, and will discuss starters and rennets — ingredients particular to making different kinds of cheeses. The following chapters will take you through descriptions of making cheeses, starting with simple cheeses like cream cheese and then working your way to the more complicated processes for making Italian cheeses, hard cheeses, and mold- and bacteria-ripened cheeses such as blue cheese and Stilton.

Part Four, like the earlier sections, will conclude with a number of different recipes that will use some of the wonderful cheese you have made. Recipes here will include cheesecake, pizza, bread, macaroni and cheese, and more.

Throughout this book, you will read case studies of people with experience in the processes of making cheese, butter, and yogurt. Some of the case studies are about people who engage in this activity at home, and others are about those who do it professionally.

Enjoy the process of making your own cheese, butter, and yogurt, and enjoy the outcome. Share it with your family and friends; they will return your gifts with smiles and praise.

PART ONE

The Home Kitchen

If you think about the fact that the production of creamery products in the home is as old as the pyramids, you can be comforted in knowing you can make many kinds of cheeses, butters, and yogurt without any high-priced kitchen gadgets. In the Old Testament, Job 10:10, it reads, "Hast thou not poured me out as milk, and curdled me like cheese?"

For many of the basic recipes in this book, the simpler you keep it, the better the finished product will be. So hold to the notion of simplicity as a mantra as you proceed.

Of course, you can purchase expensive equipment to help you make many of the products that are outlined in this book. *You will be given ideas as to where to purchase these objects in the Resources section in the back of this book.* Any craft, whether you are a bread maker or home brewer, has scores of products you can buy that may (or may not) make your job easier. But for the sake of beginners and a better understanding of the processes involved in making cheese, butter, and yogurt, this guide will try to keep things as simple as possible.

This first part of this book will detail many of the items you will come across as you get into making cheese, butter, and yogurt in your home. Some of the items are absolutely necessary to the processes, while some items can be substituted with other items. Necessary items include stainless steel pots, utensils, and a good thermometer. In contrast, you do not really need a traditional butter churn to make butter because butter can be made in a home food processor or, more simply, in a quart jar with a tight-fitting lid. You do not need a yogurt maker to make yogurt because you can make yogurt with a crock pot, a heating pad, or even an old cooler.

This first part will also detail many of the dairy products you will use to make cheese, butter, and yogurt. You will explore the various kinds of milk and cream that may be available to you and how they can be employed in your kitchen.

CHAPTER 1

Equipment

As explained earlier, you do not need a lot of fancy, expensive paraphernalia to get started making cheese, butter, and yogurt. In fact, you can make do with about four or five basic household tools. A pot, colander, slotted spoon, cheesecloth, and thermometer are all you need to get started; remember, making cheese, butter, and yogurt dates back hundreds of years before instant-read thermometers, double boilers, and specialized curd knives were used. If you find that your kitchen is not equipped with some of these items, you can find alternative ways of doing the job.

An example of specialized equipment that is a luxury and not a necessity is a $500 yogurt maker. You can pay $500 and get a nice machine that will make good yogurt, or you can keep your culturing yogurt warm with a heating pad, a crock-pot, or in a sink full of warm water. Once you learn the basic items, you will find there are often a number of different ways to accomplish what it is you need to do to achieve your desired cooking result.

Here is some of the basic equipment you will need to get started making your own cheese, butter, and yogurt:

Pots – Although you can get away with one large, stainless-steel or unchipped enamel pot, you will probably find that having several pots is much easier. The important point to make about pots is to make sure you do not use cast iron or aluminum pots with dairy products because the acidity in dairy products will react with the iron and aluminum, causing the iron and aluminum to leach into your product. Leaching means there is a chemical reaction that causes iron or aluminum to transfer from the pot or utensil into your dairy product.

Another important factor in choosing a good pot is that it has a heavy bottom. Pots with heavy reinforced bottoms allow for a more even distribution of heat. It is more convenient if you have a large double boiler. Having the ability to heat your milk in an indirect manner is a good way to keep temperatures consistent over several hours.

Make sure your pots are large enough to hold 2 to 3 gallons of liquid. If you do not have a double boiler, have several 3-gallon pots and a larger one to set them in to serve as a double boiler. The larger pot of the double boiler should be able to hold the smaller pot and some water that will be heated. Ideally, the smaller pot can sit inside the larger pot while not touching the bottom of the larger pot. You want water to be moving all around the smaller pot to allow for an even distribution of heat.

Cheesecloth – You will probably want to have two kinds of cheesecloth on hand. For some cheeses and butter, you will be able to use the cheesecloth that is readily available at your neighborhood grocery store. You will find that for soft cheese, semi-soft cheese, and butter, you will be able to use standard cheesecloth. When you proceed to aged and ripened cheese, you will want to use the professional-grade cheesecloth available through cheese-making supply houses. The recipes in the book will let you know what kind of cheesecloth you should be using and how to use it.

You will have to use a double layer of the basic cheesecloth that you buy in your grocery store. This basic cheesecloth is serviceable for butter, cream cheese, ricotta, and a number of other products. The cheesecloth you buy in the grocery store has a very loose weave, meaning that the holes in the fabric are larger than tightly woven cloth and you will lose some of the curd when you drain your product — but it is still a usable cloth. Ideally, when you strain your product, you want to separate the curd from the whey, and if the cheesecloth you use allows some of the solid curd to flow through with the whey, you need tighter-woven cheesecloth, or you need to double- or triple-layer the cloth you are using. You can purchase tighter-woven cheesecloth at cheese-making supply houses, and this product is preferable, as it catches more curd. *There is a list of supply houses in the Appendix of this book that can direct you to cheese-making suppliers.*

Butter muslin is a more tightly woven fabric than cheesecloth. The benefit to using butter muslin is that it is stronger and reusable. Also, because butter muslin is more tightly woven than cheesecloth, you will not lose curds as you drain your product.

Whether you are using cheesecloth or butter muslin, you can reuse these cloths if you first thoroughly rinse the cloth in cold water, and then wash them with bleach and hot, soapy water. You can also go the extra mile by washing them in boiling water.

Colander – A large, stainless-steel or food-grade plastic colander is preferable, but because you will be lining it with cheesecloth or butter muslin, you can use just about any kind of sturdy colander. If your colander is strong enough to strain a pound of pasta, you can use it to drain curds and whey.

Curd knife – This is not necessarily a specialized utensil but is a long, flat-bladed knife that has a rounded or flat end, as opposed to a sharp point. Make sure the blade is long enough to reach into the bottom of your large pot of milk without the handle's getting wet. The reason that curd knives do not have sharp points is because they do not need them; they are used to cut the soft curds. You can use a long knife of any kind, or even a long, flat spatula instead of purchasing this item.

Ladles – You will find two different types of ladles will come in handy. The first kind is a large, perforated ladle known as a skimmer. This is a flat, perforated tool, as opposed to a soup ladle, and it is primarily used to scoop curds from the pot and leave the whey behind. This skimmer is also good for stirring liquids such as milk and whey in your large pots. The other kind of ladle you should use is a large soup ladle. Soup ladles generally hold a ¼ to ½ cup of liquid and are good for transferring liquids from one pot to another. Both of these utensils should be stainless steel.

Measuring cup – A good 2-cup glass measuring cup is preferable, but any good quality measuring cup will work.

Measuring spoons – Again, you will want these to be stainless steel.

Thermometer – An instant-read food thermometer that ranges from 0 to 220°F and can be inserted at least a couple of inches into the milk is desirable. "Instant read" means it indicates the temperature very quickly, which is important when you are increasing the heat of milk and you need to know exactly what the temperature is in an instant. You will find that two thermometers will come in handy, as it is good to know the temperature of your milk and the temperature of water. Often, you will find that one of your thermometers might not be clean when you need it, so having a second thermometer will be useful. Also, you will find it useful if you have the kind of thermometers that can clip onto the edge of a pot. To test to see if your thermometers are accurate, boil some water and check the reading of the thermometer. If you get a reading of 212°, your tool is working properly. *Note that all recipes and directions in this book refer to temperatures using the Fahrenheit scale.*

In addition, you may want to have a notebook handy to note your successes and failures. Make note of what works, what does not work, and what you think you might be able to do differently next time. Also, once you get into making aged cheeses, it is good to note the specifics of dates you started to age a particular cheese, temperatures you aged the cheese at, or how much weight you used to press whey from the curd. There is a lot of specific information you will want to track as you learn to make cheese. *You will learn more about pressing, aging, and temperature control later in Chapter 10 and beyond.*

As you progress from making butter, yogurt, and a few of the simpler items to more advanced cheese making, you will need more specialized items. As you learn the craft and research what end result is needed, you can improvise and come up with some of your own specialized tools. Here is a list of tools that are specific to cheese making:

Molds and baskets – These hold the curds together, drain the whey, and form the cheese when it is pressed. Cheese molds and baskets should be made from stainless steel or a food-grade plastic. You can make these items out of empty plastic food containers, like sour cream, cottage cheese, or yogurt containers, by punching holes in a regular pattern to allow the whey to drain evenly as the cheese is pressed.

Draining pans – This is simply a pan that catches the whey draining off from the cheese press, basket, or mold. You can use a glass pie plate, a baking sheet, or a specialized draining pan purchased from a cheese-making supply house.

Cheese boards – Boards are also used to drain cheese. Be sure to use a good, hard-wood board such as maple or birch. Hardwood is denser and allows for minimal moisture so the bad, harmful bacteria are less likely to exist on these boards and transfer from the wood to the cheese.

Cheese mats – They are made from food-grade plastic, bamboo, or reeds, and are used to drain and dry cheese.

Cheese press – This is an item you can spend $300 dollars on — or you can use bricks, dumbbells, or a pile of old books. The press is used to expel moisture from the curds. Cheese presses are used, for the most part, when making hard cheeses such as Parmesan or cheddar. The presses apply pressure on the curds to shape them in a mold and press out the whey. In many of the cheese recipes, you will note that specific weights are used for specific amounts of time, as different cheeses have different amounts of moisture and are varied in their consistency. Drier cheese will call for more weight to press out more liquid than softer cheese, which has more moisture in it.

The cheese press consists of a basket or mold (see above); a follower that fits tightly on top of the curds and allows for even pressure to be put on them; and a method of applying weight. You need to be sure the follower fits tightly into the mold so the curd does not seep out from around the edges as pressure is applied. A follower is simply a flat disk that fits snugly inside a cheese mold to apply even pressure to the curd, like a coffee press.

There are many different kinds of cheese presses. Do a Web search of the words "cheese press" and you will find many brands and even some diagrams to make your own. Or, you can simply make your own press out of a basket, a follower you cut from food-grade plastic, and some bricks. To accomplish this, use a food-grade plastic container (a yogurt container works well), and punch a series of evenly distributed holes in it that will allow for even drainage. Find or cut a round disk that will fit snugly in the open top of the container. You do not want the disk to sit on top of the container, but to slide into the top like a piston would. Finally, you need a weight that you will place on top of the disk to press the cheese. A brick works well, as does a filled soda bottle. You place your cheesecloth-wrapped cheese curd into the container, set the follower (disk) on top of the cheese, and put the weight atop the follower.

Atomizer – You will need a spray bottle that sprays liquid as a fine mist when you get to the advanced cheese making of mold-ripened cheeses. For making mold-ripened cheese, you will use the atomizer spray bottle to lightly spray mold solution on the surface of your cheese.

Cheese wax – Wax is used to put a protective cover on aging cheese. The wax protects against unwanted bacteria and prevents the cheese from drying out during its aging process. Cheese wax is not paraffin, which is easily cracked; cheese wax is tougher, much more pliant than paraffin, and reusable.

Wax brush – This is used to brush cheese wax onto your cheese. Select a natural-bristle, 2-inch brush rather than a nylon brush, which would melt.

Wax pot – Used for melting cheese wax. Your best choice is to choose a pot that can be used as a double boiler because you will want to melt wax using this indirect method. You can choose a quart pan/pot for a 1-pound wax block or a gallon pan/pot for a 5-pound block. If you choose the larger pot, you might consider dipping your cheese in the wax as opposed to using a brush. *Waxing cheese will be discussed in greater detail later in Chapter 10.*

pH tester – Making some kinds of cheese will require you to test the acidity levels of your product. To do this, you can use a pH tester or test paper strips. When you buy pH test strips, make sure they have the pH range you will need, which should be between a 5 and a 7. If you buy test strips meant to test swimming pool water, they may not test below 6.

Cave – If you do not have a real cave in your backyard or under your house, you can consider having a dedicated refrigerator. The cave is a place where you can age your cheese at a controlled temperature and humidity level. Some cheeses do not require this, but most of the cheeses that need to be aged for several weeks to months will need to age in a cool place (usually at 50° to 55°).

Jars – You should plan on having a good supply of quart jars and tops on supply, so purchase a case of 12 jars to start with. The jars are handy to have if you plan on saving your whey, which is an excellent liquid to use in baking. They are also great to have handy for buttermilk, butter making, kefir (a cultured milk much like cultured buttermilk), or many other purposes. Also, be sure that the jars you purchase are canning-quality jars because these jars are made to stand up to heat.

Many of the items described above will be reviewed again in the coming chapters as they are called for. Also, many of their uses will become clearer. As you continue to learn more about the processes and techniques of making creamery items, you will adapt your utensils and tools for your own use. Remember, the processes described in the following chapters are centuries-old. Instant-read thermometers were not used to make cheese in the olden days; people adapted and used what they had at hand. The same will be true of many of the ingredients you will read about in the next chapter.

Now that you have your tools, you can move on to Chapter 2 for a discussion of the ingredients you will need to get started. Get your shopping list out.

CASE STUDY: MICHAEL AND ED LOBAUGH

The Old Windmill Dairy
www.theoldwindmilldairy.com

Michael Lobaugh is involved in the dairy operations of running the dairy, which includes milking the goats in the morning, making cheese, packaging, marketing, handling sales, and delivering the product. Ed Lobaugh, his business partner, is mainly involved in outside direct sales and product development. While Ed does the research and development of crafting new flavors and cheese, Michael implements the recipes and puts them into production.

Ed was strongly influenced by his grandparents, who had a small goat dairy when he was child, and Michael truly wanted to leave corporate life and become a farmer. Together, they started with what they knew about goats and milk handling. From there, Ed consulted with his grandmother. Both Michael and Ed consulted with the New Mexico Department of Agriculture, other cheese makers, and professional dairyman consultants to design their dairy and product line.

The Lobaughs always had a passion for making cheese and sharing their products with friends and family. They invested $250,000 into their new business venture and started with only two goats and a dream. Their dairy started small but grew to a herd of 40 within five years. During that time, they began making cheese in their kitchen, sometimes working from 5 a.m. to midnight. In July 2007, six years after they started, they opened their Grade A dairy. They have been a commercial dairy for nearly three years and make more than seven different cheese, including fresh and aged cheeses.

"We enjoy seeing the success of our labor. Mostly we enjoy seeing how happy people are when they eat our cheese. We get the pleasure of seeing people's eyes light up and sparkle with excitement when they taste our cheese at a local farmers' market. We also enjoy eating our own cheese. It something we always bring to a party," Michael said.

Michael said time management is the most difficult thing about making cheese. In a commercial dairy, there are many projects going on besides making cheese, such as training employees, dealing with equipment failures, and tending to your herd. As a beginner, it is a challenge to understand the steps, the linguistics, and what each ingredient does to make the end product of making cheese.

"We like to eat a finely ripened cheese. We made Romano cheese, which came out spectacularly. It has a nice, salty, dry, complex flavor that works well with tomato-based dishes. There are two other cheeses that we are very proud of, as they have both taken national blue ribbons. Our 'Chili n Hot Chèvre™' (chèvre made with New Mexico green chile, jalapeno, and garlic) and our 'Manzano Blue Moon' (a goat's milk blue cheese that is creamy on the outside and crumbly on the inside).

"We encourage beginners to take a cheese-making class from a professional. It is in this setting beginners will understand what the term 'clean break' means, how to perform a texture test, and how to salt cheese. Initially when making feta and other more advanced cheese such as Mozzarella; a cheese maker needs to understand how culture ripening affects the acidity of cheese. Developing the perfect acidity is quintessential when making feta, Mozzarella, cheddar, and Gouda. Having this basic understanding is essential to making good cheese."

CHAPTER 2

Ingredients

The wonderful thing about making creamery items such as butter, yogurt, and cheese in your home is you only need one ingredient: milk. That being said, the kind of milk you have access to is very important. Also, you will find that having access to other ingredients will greatly aid your task, especially when it comes to making cheese. But this chapter will begin by discussing milk.

Milk

If you were to read in a recipe, "add a cup of milk," what would you do? You would more than likely go to your refrigerator, take out a plastic jug, and pour a cup of milk. Now, stop and ask some questions about what you just poured. Did you just pour a cup of cow's milk? Is it skim milk, 1 percent, 2 percent, or whole milk? If it is whole milk, what is the fat content? Is it farm-fresh, pasteurized, homogenized, or ultra-pasteurized — a combination of these options?

Milk is actually quite complex. The assumption that you poured cow's milk comes from that fact that you more than likely got your milk from a local supermarket in the United States. However, you could have poured goat's milk (that is fairly readily available in the United States), sheep's milk, water buffalo's milk, camel's milk, reindeer's milk, or moose's milk. You can even use porpoise's milk, which has a whopping 45 percent fat content compared to the just under 4 percent of cow's milk. You might find the notion of porpoise's milk funny, but you would be surprised at the variety of animals people have experimented using milk from.

Most of the recipes in this book call for cow's milk, but some of the recipes call for goat's milk. This is not to say that you cannot use sheep's milk, but you will have to make a few adjustments if you do. Sheep's milk is much higher in fat content and in total solids than cow's or goat's milk. According to George F.W. Haenlein, professor emeritus of dairy science at the University of Delaware, human, cow, and goat's milk are all fairly similar with regard to the amount of solids and fat they contain. Sheep's milk, on the other hand, has a much higher fat and solid content. Because it has less water, more fat, and more solid, sheep's milk will produce a greater yield of cheese than goat's or cow's milk. Because it is so high in fat, you need to adjust the way you use it. *When you get to the chapters on making cheese (Chapter 10 and beyond), this will be explored in greater detail.*

Goat's milk is the preferred material to use in many cases because it is easier to digest than cow's milk because of smaller fat globules — the small fat globules are more readily dispersed in the milk. However, the smaller fat globules in goat's milk make it more difficult to produce butter. Though it is not impossible to make butter out of goat's milk, you will have to take a couple of extra steps. *This will be covered in greater detail in chapters 4 and 5 on making butter.*

Cow's milk is the overall milk of choice when making most recipes in this book because it is the most easily available and, for the most part, the easiest to work with. Most cheese recipes can be made with whole milk, though a number of them can also be made with skim or low-fat milk. The only kind you should avoid when you buy milk to make cheese or yogurt is ultra-pasteurized milk. Ultra-pasteurization is the extreme heating of milk to destroy what might be considered bad bacteria, but this process also destroys many of the basic components of milk — enzymes, organisms, and protein structures. Milk producers treat milk this way to give it a longer shelf life, but it is bad for the home creamery.

Homogenized milk is milk that has been heat-treated to break up fat globules. This produces a milk product that makes for a smoother curd. Also, homogenization evenly distributes the fat globules in the milk, which means that they do not rise to the top.

You may be in a location where you have more places to obtain milk than your local grocery store. You may have access to raw milk, which is not pasteurized or homogenized, so it is higher in vitamins and richer in flavor. If you would like access to raw milk, you might be able to find a close source via A Campaign for Real Milk on the Web at **www.realmilk.com/where2.html**. Click "Where" in the left-hand column, then click "Sources of Real Milk in the USA," scroll down, and click on your state. The rule of thumb in obtaining raw milk is to make sure it is free of pathogens, which are disease-causing bacteria. Reputable dairy farmers know the state of the health of their stock. Overall, there is strict oversight of raw milk producers, and most states monitor the safety of raw milk production on a monthly basis at minimum. If you are dealing with a reputable farmer, you will probably be all right. It helps to know the farmer's operations, and if in doubt, pasteurize the milk yourself.

How to Pasteurize Milk

1. Using a stainless steel pot, set up a double boiler on a stovetop.

2. Heat the milk to 150° F and hold it at this temperature for 30 minutes. Monitor the temperature with an instant-read or dairy thermometer. If the temperature is lower, the milk will not be properly pasteurized. If the temperature is higher, it will destroy the protein in the milk. If the protein is destroyed, the curd will not set properly for cheese making.

3. After 30 minutes, remove the milk from the double boiler and put the pot of milk immediately into a sink full of ice water that is the same level as the milk in the pot.

4. Stir the milk constantly until it reaches 40° F; this removes the warm conditions in which bacteria might grow, which is the goal of pasteurization.

5. Refrigerate the milk.

Whole milk is milk that has all of its fat content. You can, in some places, still buy whole milk that has cream on the top. *Cream will be discussed in more detail a little later in this chapter.* Whole cow's milk has a butterfat content of between 3.5 and 4 percent. Milk that is labeled 1 percent or 2 percent has that corresponding amount of butterfat. Skim (nonfat) milk has a butterfat content of less than 1 percent because most of the butterfat has been removed. You can still make cheese or yogurt with skim milk, even though it has had most of the fat removed. Skim milk will give a lower yield of cheese, but you will still be able to make fine-tasting cheese and yogurt from skim milk.

Dry milk powder, or dehydrated milk solids, can be used to make a number of creamery and cheese products. A common use of dry milk powder is to thicken the milk to be used for yogurt, buttermilk, or sour cream. You can also use dry milk powder to make a number of soft cheeses. *There are directions on how to do these things in the specific recipes found in chapters 5, 7, 8, and 9.*

Cream

Cream is the fat that rises to the top of whole cow's milk. For nearly all recipes that call for cream, you want the best cream available, which is heavy, pasteurized cream. Heavy cream means the fat content is about 40 percent. Whipping cream has a fat content of about 30 percent; light cream has a fat content of 20 to 30 percent; and half and half has a fat content of 10 to 18 percent. Half and half will not whip, but the other creams will. *Learn more about cream in the chapters on butter (chapters 4 through 6).*

There are a few creamery items that can be made using only milk or cream. You can make butter and true buttermilk with only cream, and soured milk can produce several types of cheese, such as pot cheese and farmer's cheese. *See Chapter 11 for more on how to make these cheeses.* To make the rest of the products in this book, you will need a few more key ingredients: cultures, rennets, and acids.

Cultures

When making dairy products, cultures refer to milk bacteria. You will often hear them referred to as starter cultures because the milk bacteria are used to start the growth of the bacteria that turns milk to cheese, yogurt, buttermilk, and a number of other creamery products. The bacterium, when added to the milk, makes the milk more acidic and consumes the lactose, producing a by-product called lactic acid. The longer the culture grows, the more acid is produced. This acid sours the milk and allows curd to form, which is the first step in producing cheese.

There are two types of starter cultures in making cheese: mesophilic and thermophilic.

Mesophilic cultures are low-temperature cultures that can survive up to 102° and are usually used when the curds are not heated above that temperature. Buttermilk, Gouda, Colby, and feta are examples of items made with mesophilic culture.

Thermophilic cultures can thrive up to 132° and are usually used when the curds are not heated over that temperature. Yogurt, Mozzarella, and Swiss cheese are examples of items made using thermophilic cultures.

When you use a culture, you will use it in one of two manners: as a mother culture or as a direct-set culture. A direct-set culture is a prepackaged culture you can purchase from a cheese-making supply house. It eliminates the need to go through the lengthy process of making a mother culture. For the beginner cheese maker, it is simplest to purchase packets of a direct-set starter culture. These will come as pre-measure starters that are kept frozen and are good for a single use as you make cheese. You will use either mesophilic or thermophilic starters, depending on the kind of cheese you are making.

Once you get into advanced cheese making, you may consider developing your own mother cultures. Using mother cultures is the traditional way of making many creamery items like buttermilk, yogurt, and cheese.

How to Create a Mother Culture

Not all mother cultures are created equal. Some cultures are serial cultures and can be kept going continuously if handled properly. A good example of a serial culture is a buttermilk culture. Once you properly culture buttermilk, the product you make will become the mother culture, and by re-moving a small amount of the buttermilk each time you make it, you will be able to create more buttermilk. Other cultures, such as kefir cultures, can usually create about seven generations of kefir before you will need to re-culture a new batch.

Below you will find directions on making several different types of mother cultures. The first couple of steps are the same for each culture.

1.   Obtain, from a cheese-making supply house, a starter for the type of culture you will be making. There are mesophilic and thermophilic cultures, but within each of these designations are numerous types of cultures that will be used to make specific kinds of cheese. There are resources noted in the back of this book that will guide you to Web sites that sell starter cultures you can use to make a mother culture.

2. Be sure all of your equipment is sterile. To make a single batch of mother culture, place a clean, 1-quart canning jar and lid in boiling water for five minutes to sterilize it.

Buttermilk

3. Heat 1 quart of milk (whole or skim) in a double boiler to 185°. Hold at 185° for 30 minutes, stirring often.
4. Remove from heat and let cool to 77°. It is beneficial to do this quickly by placing the pan in a sink full of cold water.
5. Gently stir ⅛ tsp freeze-dried buttermilk culture (obtained from a cheese-making supply house) into milk and pour into sterilized 1-quart jar. Cover loosely.
6. Allow cultured milk to remain at room temperature (72° - 77°) for 15 to 18 hours.
7. Refrigerate.

You now have about 1 quart of cultured buttermilk; this is your mother culture. You will use ¾ cup to make your next quart-sized batch of buttermilk. You should use the culture within a week's time to keep the culture active.

Mesophilic starter

3. Fill the sterilized jar to about ½ inch from the rim with skim milk.
4. Put the jar in a deep pot of boiling water so the jar is submersed. It is a good idea to have a rack in the bottom of the water pot so the jar of milk is not sitting directly on the pot.
5. Let the jar remain in the boiling water for 30 minutes.
6. Use tongs to remove the jar from the boiling water, and let it cool to room temperature (about 72°). Check the jar's temperature with an instant-read thermometer. Do not open the jar while it is cooling, as you may invite unwanted bacteria into your starter.
7. When the jar has cooled to about 72°, open it and add your mesophilic starter. Immediately close the jar and shake it lightly to mix the starter into the milk. *(If you are regenerating a mother culture, add 2 ounces of mother culture to the jar.)*
8. Let the closed jar sit at room temperature for 16 to 24 hours; the culture will appear yogurt-like in consistency.
9. Refrigerate and use or freeze within three days.

10. To freeze your mother culture, you can place it in sterilized ice cube trays, wrap the trays in plastic, and freeze them. Each "cube" is about 1 ounce. Once the cubes are frozen, you can remove them from the tray and place them in resealable freezer bags.

11. Thaw cubes of culture prior to using to make cheese or another starter batch.

Thermophilic starter

Follow the first two points as described above (obtain starter and sterilize jars).

3.   Fill the sterilized jar to about ½ inch from the jar's rim with skim milk.

4.   Put the jar in a deep pot of boiling water so the jar is submersed. It is a good idea to have a rack in the bottom of the water pot so the jar of milk is not sitting directly on the pot.

5.   Let the jar remain in the boiling water for 30 minutes.

6.   Remove the jar from the boiling water and let it cool to 110°. Check the temperature with your instant-read thermometer. Do not open the jar while it is cooling.

7.   When the jar has cooled to about 110°, open it and add your thermophilic starter. Immediately close the jar and shake it lightly to mix the starter into the milk. *(If you are regenerating a mother culture, add 2 ounces of mother culture to the jar.)*

8.   Let the closed jar incubate at 110° for six to eight hours. A good way to achieve this and hold the temperature steady is to use a crock pot with a warm setting. Another option is to wrap the jar with a heating pad. The culture will appear yogurt-like in consistency.

9.   Refrigerate and use or freeze before three days.

10. To freeze your mother culture, you can place it in sterilized ice cube trays, wrap the trays in plastic, and freeze them. Each "cube" is about 1 ounce. Once the cubes are frozen, you can remove them from the tray and place them in resealable freezer bags.

11. Thaw cubes of culture prior to using to make cheese or another starter batch.

Rennet

Rennet is an enzyme that aids in the coagulation of milk. It comes in several forms and is derived from an animal or vegetable source. You can use liquid rennet or buy it in tablet form. It is believed the earliest cheese making began when people stored milk in the stomachs of goats. They noticed the milk would readily curdle when stored in this manner due to the rennet that is naturally found in the stomach. The animal rennet available for use today is generally from calves and is a by-product of veal production. Vegetable rennet is derived from any one of a number of plants such as nettle, butterwort, mallow, or yarrow. You can find many of these plants at a local garden center, and you can make your own rennet by crushing the plant with a large mortar and pestle, and straining the resulting liquid. Most vegetable rennet you can purchase today is from the mold *Mucor miehei.*

There are benefits and drawbacks to each type of rennet, and as you progress in making cheese, you will discover which one works best for you. When you first start making cheese, you will probably want to choose vegetable rennet in tablet form because the tablets have a longer shelf life than the liquid form. If you store the tablets in an airtight container in the freezer, you can count on their potency for a couple of years. Liquid rennet is measured more precisely than tablets and will keep in the refrigerator for about a year. The tablets usually come marked to be cut into quarters. You will find you will rarely use an entire tablet with any batch of cheese you make (usually you will only use ¼ or ½ tablet). The tablets often will fall apart as you cut them, and there will be some waste.

If you or anyone you will be sharing cheese with is a vegetarian, you will want to opt for the vegetable rennet. As you advance in your cheese making and learn how various rennets may alter the taste and consistency of your product, you may choose animal rennet, but as a beginner, the vegetable form in tablet is best, as it is easiest to measure and will keep longer in your freezer.

To use rennet, whether you are using a tablet or the liquid, you should dissolve the tablet or dilute the liquid in about ¼ cup of unchlorinated, cool water. (Chlorinated water can destroy the enzyme action of the rennet.) The water allows the rennet to be well-dispersed throughout the milk. If the rennet is not evenly distributed, you will wind up with a curd that is not properly formed, as it will be uneven and lumpy. If you are using powdered or tablet rennet, allow the powder or tablet to sit in the cool, unchlorinated water for 20 to 30 minutes to be sure that the powder or tablet is completely dissolved.

Calcium Chloride

Calcium chloride is an optional ingredient in cheese making but is quite beneficial to settle the curd. If you are using farm-fresh milk, you will not need to use calcium chloride. Calcium chloride is used on store-bought milk that has been through the process of homogenization and high-temperature pasteurization. These processes harm the calcium balance in the milk and have a negative impact on the enzyme action of the rennet used to form the curd. The suggested use of calcium chloride is about ⅛ tsp diluted in ¼ cup of cool, unchlorinated water.

Molds and Bacteria

These are what make blue cheese blue and make the holes in Swiss cheese. Some bacteria are mixed into the ripening milk, and some are sprayed on the surface of cheese and allowed to creep into the cheese over time. Mold is a parasitic life form that requires a host to survive, and cheese (because of its large amount of protein and moisture) is a perfect host. Making mold- and bacteria-ripened cheese is the most time-consuming and advanced stage of cheese making. It is better if you are well-studied and confident in basic cheese making before you venture into this area.

Some of the basic bacteria used to make cheese are:

- *Penicillium candidum* – This a white mold that is most commonly used as a surface mold on Brie. This is the mold that gives Brie its white coat. The mold helps the flavor of the cheese as it ages and gives it texture as well. If you tasted Brie made without *Penicillium candidum*, it would be extremely sour and rubbery.

- ***Penicillium roqueforti*** – A blue mold used in such cheeses as Gorgonzola and blue cheese. *Penicillium roqueforti* is a surface mold that creeps into the cheese during the aging process.

- ***Geotrichum candidum*** – This is another white mold that is used together with *Penicillium candidum* in the aging of Camembert and Brie.

- ***Brevibacterium linens*** – A red bacteria used on cheeses that are surface-washed. Surface washing is a process that some cheeses must go through on a regular basis as it ages. The washing helps distribute the bacteria evenly over the surface of the cheese. Cheeses such as Muenster, Limburger, and brick are aged using *Brevibacterium linens*.

- ***Propionibacterium shermanii*** – This is the bacteria used to give Swiss cheese its smooth flavor and holes. *Propionibacterium shermanii* is blended into the milk early in the cheese-making process.

There are many other molds and bacteria you can use in this advanced cheese making. As you learn and become more knowledgeable about the techniques and processes of aging cheese, you will come to know many more specialty molds and bacteria. Most of the molds and bacteria listed above can be kept in the freezer for up to six months, except for *Penicillium roqueforti*, which cannot be frozen but can be refrigerated for up to six months.

Lipase

Lipase is an optional ingredient that is used primarily in making Italian cheeses such as Mozzarella, Parmesan, and provolone. Lipase is an enzyme that will make a stronger-flavored cheese when added to milk. Lipase comes in powdered form and can be stored in the freezer for about six months.

Cheese Salt

This is a flaked, non-iodized salt that is used to enhance the flavor of a number of different cheeses, such as Mozzarella, cottage cheese, and Parmesan. You can also use cheese salt to make the brine for soaking cheeses that require a brine, such as Mozzarella. You do not need to use specialty cheese salt; a good, non-iodized kosher salt will serve the same purpose. Do not use an iodized salt, as iodine will inhibit the growth of the bacteria necessary to make cheese.

Unchlorinated Water

If you live in an area where your tap water is chlorinated, you will want to buy unchlorinated water. Chlorine will affect the action of the rennet, and your milk will not coagulate; that is, it will not form into a thickened mass.

Acids

You will usually use only rennet to promote coagulation in your milk, but there are times when you can rely on various acids to do the trick. Citric acid, vinegar, tartaric acid, or citrus juices such as lemon juice are used in various cheese recipes such as lemon cheese, mascarpone, and Mozzarella.

You can find most of the specialty products listed above at cheese supply stores and Web sites that are listed in the Resources section at the back of this book. Now that you have all the ingredients necessary, we will discuss the process of making butter.

CASE STUDY: CAITLIN OWEN HUNTER

Appleton Creamery
www.appletoncreamery.com

Appleton Creamery is a small-scale family farm located in scenic mid-coast Maine. Caitlin and Bradley Hunter tend a herd of Alpine dairy goats, hand-crafting cheese daily using traditional methods and marketing it throughout the mid-coast area through farmers' markets, restaurants, and stores. Caitlin has been making cheese and raising goats since 1979. She and Bradley started running Appleton Creamery in 1990, first as a hobby and then commercially in 1994.

"We make cheese from goat's milk, sheep's milk from EllsFarm in nearby Union, and cow's milk from Grassland Dairy in Skowhegan. We make butter when we can source the cow's cream, and yogurt from the sheep's milk. Most of our sales are directly to our customers, and we don't distribute out of state," Caitlin said."We were both back-to-the-landers in the 1970s, when raising your own livestock was part of small-scale farming. When you have goats, you need to find a way to support them, and cheese making came naturally to us. We aren't interested in showing and don't have the land base to pasture raise surplus animals for meat. We are also fortunate enough to live in an area rich with farmers' markets and good restaurants, and the annual cycle of demand matches the goat's seasons."

"I love tending the animals that provide the milk for our dairy products. I love the entire farm cycle: animal to product, to bringing it to the consumer. I love the magic of transforming the same raw material, milk, into a dazzling array of cheeses simply by manipulating time, temperature, and curd," she said.

Caitlin said the hardest part about making cheese was trying to learn from a book. She encourages hands-on experience, either by interning with a dairy or cheese maker, or taking classes. She said she will never stop taking classes. Her favorite cheese to make is chèvre, but she enjoys eating a nicely aged, bloomy-rind ashed goat cheese.

"For those who are just getting started in making cheese: Keep practicing. Get chickens to eat your mistakes. Give cheese to all your friends to try. Educate yourself about cheese by eating a lot of cheese."

PART TWO

Butter

Making butter is the best place to start as you begin to learn and understand how to transform milk and cream into wonderful creamery items. If you have children, getting them involved in making butter can be fun and quite educational. One of the great things about the simple act of making butter is you will gain confidence in the creamery-making process. Once you see your creamery mixture turn into butter, you will be astounded by your abilities. When you spread that butter on your homemade bread or use it in a recipe, you will recognize the superiority of your homemade product. After you learn the basics of making butter, you will soon be able to make buttermilk, crème fraiche, yogurt, and cheese.

CHAPTER 3

Spreading the Word on Butter

When you stand in the dairy aisle of your local supermarket and look at the refrigerator case where the butter is kept, it is amazing that something as simple as butter can come in so many different varieties. You can get raw-cream butter, sweet-cream butter, lightly salted butter, salted butter, blended butter (with peanut oil, canola oil, olive oil, or vegetable oil), or whipped butter. You can get butter with omega-3 fatty acids, flax seed, fish oil, plant sterols, and stenols — sterols and stenols are naturally occurring substances found in plants that fight against cholesterol buildup. All these butter options can make your head spin.

The best butter you will ever taste may be the butter you make at home. Butter is such a simple food that once you make it yourself, you may have a hard time justifying staring down the dairy case ever again.

Butter has been used for at least 4,000 years. It is even mentioned in the Old Testament: "She brought forth butter in a lordly dish" (Judges 5:25). This is generally believed to have been recorded in 650 BC. The word "butter" comes from the Greek word *bouturo*, which means "cow cheese."

It is speculated that butter was first discovered when warm milk was inadvertently churned as it was being transported from place to place. Stories have been told about farmers who placed an amount of milk in a saddlebag before they rode to town so by the time they returned home, the milk was churned to butter.

Barrels of garlic butter dating back 1,000 years have been found under the peat bogs of Ireland. Some of these Irish barrels have weighed in at more than 100 pounds.

Until about 300 years ago, butter production was something that was strictly done in the home. Most cultures that raised domesticated animals had a source of milk and the ability to produce their own dairy products. Dairy farmers began to produce butter on a large scale by the mid-1700s in Europe. At this time, butter produced by these dairy farmers was considered a luxury item as the farmers molded their particular butter in specially shaped molds. Butter stamps shaped in fancy patterns decorated larger blocks and rounds of butter.

The Industrial Revolution of the 19th century moved much of the butter production from the farm to the factory. During this time period, the large-scale factory replaced the small-scale creamery, which is where the farmer converted cream into butter. As industrialization swept Europe, the function of the creamery changed. The creamery became a place where all milk was brought to be turned into butter and cheese. Industrialization meant convenience. Creameries continued to operate at this time, but their function and output was different and decreased.

The manufacture and use of butter remained fairly constant for most of the 19th century, but in the 1870s butter manufacturing was dealt a mighty blow by Emperor Louis Napoleon III when he offered a prize for whoever came up with a good substitute for butter. He created this competition because the growing demand for butter could not be kept. Chemist Hippolyte Mège-Mouriez formulated a new substance out of a fatty acid called margaric acid and won the emperor's prize. This substance came to be known as margarine.

Since that time, margarine has battled butter for the taste buds of the consumer. You cannot make margarine at home. Make butter at home and you will not be tempted by margarine, let alone store-bought butter, again. You will not only have great-tasting, fresh butter by making it at home, but you have the byproduct of true buttermilk, which is not available in any store anywhere.

As you begin to make your homemade butter, know that what you are doing has essentially been done in the same manner for more than 4,000 years. If you have children or younger family members, you can get them involved and give them a bit of a fun and tasty history lesson. Making butter can also be considered the makings of a great science experiment. As you are churning cream to butter, think about all of the great uses for your butter. There are many recipes included in these chapters; try them all. Do not be afraid to create your own butter recipes as you enjoy this simple yet delicious food.

Once you have successfully made your first batch of butter, be sure to share it with others. Bringing homemade butter to a neighbor is a great way to spread a little goodness, happiness, and neighborly warmth.

CHAPTER 4

How to Make Butter

There are dozens of ways to make butter. This chapter will describe a couple of ways for you to get started, then you can take over and have some fun by discovering more ways. One of the great things about making basic butter is you do it with one ingredient — cream. Go back to Chapter 2 and the discussion about the various kinds of cream that are available to you. You will recall that any kind of cream is suitable for making butter, but you cannot make butter with half and half. The type of cream you choose will determine the yield of butter, and the higher the fat content, the greater the butter yield, which is why you will probably want to start with heavy cream.

Making Basic Butter

Ingredient(s)

Heavy cream (not ultra-pasteurized)

Because you need only one ingredient, it does not matter how much heavy cream you use; the more cream you churn, the more butter you will get.

Salt (optional)

Most people are used to eating lightly salted butter, but salt is not necessary for making butter. Whether you add salt to your butter should be determined by your tastes and what you plan to do with the butter. If you plan on using the butter to cook or bake with, you may want to omit the salt, as many recipes call for unsalted butter.

Other possible additions to this basic butter recipe will be described later in this chapter.

Directions

1. Pour the cream into a jar with a tight-fitting lid. For the best results, the cream should be about 60°. If the cream is coming from your chilled refrigerator, remove it and allow it to sit out until it reaches the desired temperature. If the cream is at room temperature, you can refrigerate it until it reaches the desired temperature. Make sure the jar is not full to the top, as you are going to be shaking the jar, and the cream will need room to move.

2. When the lid to the jar is on tight, shake the jar for about ten minutes. As you shake, you will notice the cream will go through several changes. The cream will foam and become whipped cream. Keep shaking; small solids will start to appear. You will notice that larger, pale-yellow solids are forming.

3. When the pale yellow solids appear, you can stop shaking. Looking into the jar, you will notice that a bit of separation has occurred. You will see the pale yellow solid and a cloudy liquid; the liquid is true buttermilk. This is not the same cultured buttermilk that you buy in the store or that you will make in Chapter 5.

4. Let the jar sit for about five minutes. During this time, the solids will continue to separate from the buttermilk.

5. Put a fine screen sieve over a bowl and pour the buttermilk and solids mixture into it. The buttermilk will flow through the sieve, and the solids will be left behind.

6. Pour the buttermilk (liquid) again through a doubled piece of cheese-cloth. Retain the solids left behind and add them to the solids left in the sieve. Retain the buttermilk; you can use this later to drink or cook with.

7. Put the solids into a food-grade plastic or stainless-steel colander and rinse them with cold water. As you rinse the solids, they will start to firm up. This sounds counter-intuitive, but it is a good way to get the butter into a condition that is easy to work with.

8. Gently knead the solids with a wooden spoon. A good way to do this is to gently work the solids between two large, wooden spoons. As you do this, you will notice that you continue to work liquid out of the solids. You can just as easily perform this action in a bowl or on a flat surface. The important thing is to work as much liquid out of the solids as possible. The reason you are working the liquid out of the solids is because butter that has too much liquid in it will spoil quicker.

9. Continue to knead the butter until most of the liquid has run off, which will take between five and ten minutes. The solids will start to look more like the butter you are familiar with as it gets thicker and denser.

10. Put the butter into a bowl and knead it a couple of more minutes to make sure you have gotten all the liquid out. Some liquid may still separate at this point; you can pour that off.

11. If you are going to add salt, this is the time to do it. Knead salt in to taste. If you began with 1 pint of heavy cream, you might add ¼ tsp of salt. Do this a little at a time so you do not over-salt.

12. You can use the butter immediately or chill it in the refrigerator. Keep the butter refrigerated in a covered bowl. *More about storing butter will be discussed later in this chapter.*

This is the simplest recipe for making butter. This is a recipe kids love to take part in, and you will appreciate their love of shaking the jar. One caution, however:

Make sure that they shake the jar in a place where if the jar is dropped, it will not break all over the floor. Overzealous shaking is good for making butter, but it is easy to drop the jar.

Making Butter in a Food Processor

Ingredient(s)
1 quart of heavy cream (best results are when the cream is about 60°)
Salt (optional)

Directions

1. Pour the cream into a food processor fitted with a stainless steel blade.

2. Process the cream on high until solids appear. The cream will go through several stages before the liquid separates from the solids. Using a food processor, the solids will appear as grains about the size of rice; this process can take anywhere from two to eight minutes. Keep a close eye on the process; you can stop the food processor to check out the progress without ruining your effort.

3. After the liquid and solids have separated, let the butter sit for about five minutes. Again, the liquid that separates is true buttermilk.

4. Pour the liquid and solids through a strainer placed over a bowl.

5. Strain the liquid and butter mixture again through a double layer of cheesecloth.

6. Put the strained butter in a stainless-steel or food-grade plastic colander and knead it with a wooden spoon to work out as much liquid as you can. (You will not be rinsing the butter in this recipe.)

7. If you plan on adding salt, this is the time to do it. If you began with 1 quart of cream, you will want to use as much as ½ tsp of salt. Add the salt a little at a time to taste.

8. Knead the butter until it is a consistency you like, remembering that butter is softer when it is warm and will firm up when you refrigerate it.

9. At this point, you can put the butter in a container with a lid, or you can shape it as you wish. Historically, butter makers were known for fanciful shapes that signify the wonder of this great food. Have fun with your options.

Those are two very basic ways of making simple butter. The main idea is to agitate heavy cream until the solids separate from the buttermilk. In each of the basic recipes here, note that near the end of the process, you add salt if your taste is inclined in that direction. Here is where you can use your imagination and be creative with your butter. You might remember the garlic butter mentioned earlier that was found in Ireland. If you enjoy garlic butter, you might add garlic when it comes time to add the salt. The amount and type of garlic you add is a matter of preference and experimentation. You can also add a small amount of honey to make honey butter. With this simple butter recipe, you can be creative and have fun, adding small amounts of ingredients that will make this special food even more fun and tasty.

After you have made your butter, you have several options when it comes to storage. How you store it is determined, to some extent, by when and how you plan on using it. Are you going to use it within a week? If you made more than 1 pound of butter, you will probably want to freeze some of it. If you are going to make a pastry with the butter, you may want to freeze it. Good butter pastry starts with frozen or very cold butter.

You worked out as much of the liquid as possible as a way to lengthen the butter's shelf life; too much liquid will cause the butter to grow rancid much faster. Adding a little salt in the butter will also slow the spoilage. You will know if butter has gone rancid, as it will have a very unpleasant smell. If this occurs, throw it out.

Butter should not be stored at room temperature but in the refrigerator. If you like your butter soft and spreadable, you can remove butter from the refrigerator ten minutes before you plan on using it. Butter should be protected from heat, light, and air as much as possible. When you keep your butter in the refrigerator, keep a lid on it. Keep the butter away from foods with odors if you do not cover it because butter will absorb those odors.

Most refrigerators have butter drawers or butter keepers. You can keep your home-made butter in the refrigerator at no more than 40° for up to a week. If you do not plan on using butter within a few days, you should freeze it. To freeze butter, wrap it in wax paper or plastic wrap before placing it in a freezer bag. Again, it is important you protect the butter from absorbing any odors. You can also place your homemade butter in a plastic container with a lid. It is suggested, however, that you also put it in a freezer bag before putting it in the freezer. Butter can be frozen for about six months. To use butter that has been frozen, thaw it overnight in the refrigerator.

Troubleshooting Butter

Because butter is so basic and quite easy to make, there are very few things that can go wrong when you make it. It is not fool-proof, though.

If you are having a hard time getting solids to form, the cream may have been either too warm or too cold. The ideal cream temperature to churn butter is 60°.

If you began with 60° cream and are still having trouble getting solids to form, your cream may not have had a high enough level of butterfat. The fat content of cream should be at least 36 percent. *See the descriptions of fat content in types of cream in Chapter 2.*

If your freshly made butter has a funny taste, you may have used un-clean utensils in making your butter. Make sure all of your utensils have been sterilized.

If your butter grows rancid very quickly, you may not have worked out enough of the liquid as you were preparing and rinsing your butter. Ran-cid butter will have a sour smell and taste that some have likened to a cross between soap and blue cheese. Do not eat rancid butter.

CASE STUDY: ERAN WAJSWOL

Valley Shepherd Creamery
www.njcheese.com

"I have been making cheese, butter, and yogurt on a daily basis for 12 years. I learned how to do it from friends in Europe 12 years ago. I have been doing it commercially part-time for six years and full-time for six years. What I enjoy most about making cheese, butter, or yogurt is the Zen of a day in the production room when everything is humming along. The hardest thing about making cheese is the seven-days-per-week schedule for eight months.

"My favorite cheese to make is our crema de blue. My favorite cheese to eat is any of our 24 cheeses as they get released from the cave… at cave temperature. My advice to those who are just getting started in making cheese is to figure out what you can sell to whom and at what price before you start making it."

CHAPTER 5

Beyond Basic Butter

Once you have mastered the technique of churning simple butter, you can begin to explore the complexities this wonderful substance can offer. In this chapter, you will learn how to make variations of butter and learn a few recipes that will incorporate the butter you have made. Also included in this chapter are a number of simple recipes that will produce creamery items from many of the same basic ingredients used to make butter — cream and a little salt or another simple ingredient. You will find that once you take the simple step just beyond butter, a world of creamery products will open up before you.

Cultured Butter

This is really your first step on your way to making cheese. Adding a culture to a dairy product is the basic idea behind yogurt, cheese, and many other foods that you will learn about in this book. You will begin by culturing butter because, like making basic butter, it is the simplest of recipes. Cultured butter is used in much the same manner as regular butter. The use of cultured butter, like salted butter, is a matter of taste preference.

A culture is a lactic acid culture that is added to dairy products such as milk and cream for the development of particular flavors and to aid in the curdling of the milk or cream. Cultures work to change the milk sugar to lactic acid in a process that is referred to as ripening.

For this recipe, you can use plain yogurt as your culture. Try to use yogurt that has no additives; the ingredients on the yogurt should read "cultured milk."

The cultures in yogurt are *Streptococcus thermophilus, Lactobacillus acidophilus, bifidus, Lactobacillus bulgaris*, and sometimes others.

Ingredients
1 quart fresh heavy cream
A culture

Directions

1. Add ⅓ cup yogurt to 1 quart of heavy cream in a clean glass or stainless steel bowl. Whisk the mixture and cover it with a tight-fitting lid.

2. Let the mixture sit at room temperature (about 72°) for about 12 hours. It will look a little thicker than when you began by this point.

3. At this point, you can follow either of the basic butter recipes in the previous chapter.

If you made this cultured butter after you made basic butter, you will find the difference in taste quite interesting. Also, you will notice a difference in the taste of the buttermilk by-product. The tastes will differ from regular butter in that they will be stronger and a bit more sour. The word best used to describe the taste might be "ripe."

This recipe will be slightly different depending on what you used to culture the cream. You can try to culture the cream with cultured buttermilk (there is a recipe for this later in this chapter), or you can experiment with other cultures. *There is a short list of cultures you might use in Chapter 7 on yogurt.*

A particularly interesting culture you can try is called piima (pronounced pee-ma). Piima is the extract from an herb called butterwort and is native to Northern Europe, particularly Scandinavian countries. Piima is quite similar in nature to buttermilk and kefir cultures. You probably will not find piima is your neighborhood grocery store, but you can find it online. *Look in the Resource directory in the back of the book for locations.*

If you choose to make cultured butter with a buttermilk culture, piima, or just about any other culture you might try, the directions are the same as the basic directions given for cultured butter. You may find in your experimentation that you have to let some cultures ripen longer or shorter periods of time than others. The best way to test how ripe your cream has grown is to smell and taste it because the product will develop a sour or acidic tartness that will increase as the product ripens.

If your cultured butter tastes "off" or somewhat too cheesy, you may have let it ripen a bit too long, or your utensils may not have been properly sterilized. Next time, keep a sharp eye on the ripening time and the cleanliness of your equipment.

There is a slight misconception about the next two recipes, clarified butter and ghee. It is sometimes thought that ghee is another word for clarified butter, but that is not the case. Clarified butter, also called drawn butter, is butter that contains only butterfat. In other words, the milk solids and water have been removed from the butter. Ghee is clarified butter that goes through the additional process of extra cooking to remove even more moisture. This extra cooking works to brown, or caramelize, the solids that are then strained out of the product.

There are many uses for both clarified butter and ghee. The first thing you might think of when you think about what to do with clarified butter is to enjoy it with lobster or any other shellfish.

Clarified butter is thought to be preferred for sautéing because it has a higher smoke point; that is, it will withstand higher temperatures before it starts to smoke. When you sauté with regular butter, what causes the smoke is the solid in butter, so when the solid is removed, you can cook at higher temperatures. This is beneficial for foods that you might want to sauté hot and fast, like shrimp.

Clarified Butter

Ingredients
Unsalted butter (1 pound of butter will yield 1 ½ cups of clarified butter)

You can use a heavy-bottomed sauce pan, but a double boiler is suggested so as not to burn the butter. A double boiler is also safer for this operation.

Directions
1. Melt the butter over a low heat. Continue cooking after the butter has melted.

2. As the butter cooks, you will notice it will separate into three layers. The top layer is water that will cook off; the middle layer is the butterfat; and the bottom layer is the milk solids.

3. After about 30 minutes, most of the water on the top will have cooked off. You will notice the color of the product has become a golden yellow, and it is a bit more transparent than it was earlier in the heating process.

4. Remove from heat and let sit for ten minutes to allow more of the solids to sink to the bottom.

5. The solids are removed at this point. You can strain the hot butter through a doubled piece of cheesecloth. Another way to remove the solids is to pour

the product into a dish and chill it. After it solidifies, you can scrape the solids from the bottom of the solidified mass.

Ghee

Ghee is a clarified butter that is cooked longer than a regular clarified butter. The extra cooking gives ghee a somewhat nutty flavor. The process of making ghee is the same as for clarified butter, but you will continue to cook the butter until the solids turn light brown. After this additional cooking, you can proceed to strain the butter.

Ghee is often associated with Indian cooking. Ghee, like clarified butter, is wonderful to use for a sauté. For example:

Ghee Vegetable Sauté

Ingredients
6 tbsp ghee
1 tsp cumin seeds
1 tsp mustard seeds
½ tsp ground black pepper
4 crushed cardamom pods
¼ tsp coarse kosher salt
Small, diced red onion
Crushed garlic cloves to taste

This is the basic sauté. Into this you can add a combination of seasonal vegetables, such as broccoli, sugar peas, potatoes, or thinly sliced summer squash.

Directions
1. In a sauté pan, heat the ghee over medium heat.
2. Add mustard seeds and cover the pan as the seeds pop (about 30 seconds).
3. Add the rest of the sauté ingredients in order of recipe.

4. When the onions start to become translucent and the garlic just begins to brown, add vegetables. If you are using broccoli, add it last, as you only want to lightly heat it.

5. Keep the vegetables moving in the pan so as not to burn them and to evenly coat them with the sauté.

6. Heat to taste.

Buttermilk

In this chapter, there have been several mentions of "true buttermilk," which is the liquid that remains after the solids have formed as cream is churned into butter. However, there is not really a consensus as to what true buttermilk is. Some will say the liquid described here is not "true buttermilk," as it is not ripened or cultured.

This true buttermilk is a product you will probably never find in a store, and you can use this liquid for drinking, baking, and cooking. You will be pleased with its taste and what it does to your baked goods, as it acts like a dough conditioner, making your breads and cakes more tender. Try buttermilk pancakes, chocolate cake, or even chocolate buttermilk beet cake.

If you would like cultured buttermilk, you need to obtain a culture (or starter) that you add to milk to help the milk ripen. You can buy cultured buttermilk in many grocery stores, but if you are a purist, you will want to make your own. Look at the ingredients on a carton of cultured buttermilk and you may be convinced you should make your own because there are probably many ingredients in that carton that you do not need.

One of the greatest benefits of culturing your own buttermilk is once you do it, you will never have to buy buttermilk again. Buttermilk is ripened by a serial culture, which means you can continue to reculture milk using a little of your previous batch. You can do this with cultured products such as buttermilk, yogurt, and kefir.

You can get buttermilk cultures through creamery and cheese supply stores. *Some online resources for these items can be found in the Resource section of this book.* When you purchase a buttermilk starter, you will have several options available to you. The various buttermilk starters differ in the amount of lactic acid that they produce, and some starters will give you a slightly stronger tasting and thicker buttermilk than others. No matter which culture you purchase, you will be happy with the final product if you prepare your culture correctly.

Preparing Buttermilk from a Starter Culture

Depending on where you obtain your starter, you will get your culture in a pre-measured packet or in a jar of culture. When you receive your culture, you should put it directly into the freezer. If the culture arrives in a jar, you will need to use about ⅛ tsp for each quart to ½ gallon of milk you plan to culture.

Ingredients

1 quart or ½ gallon of milk (You can use any kind of whole, low-fat, or skim milk as long as it is not ultra-pasteurized)

1 packet or ⅛ tsp of buttermilk culture (If you are using a premeasured packet, follow packet direction regarding the amount of milk to use)

¼ to ½ cup dry non-fat milk powder (optional)

Directions

1. In a double-boiler, heat milk to 185° and keep it at that temperature for at least 30 minutes.

2. If you are using the dry milk, you can whisk it in as you heat the milk. The milk powder is made up of milk solids that will give your buttermilk more body while not adding any fat.

3. Let the milk cool to about 78°. You can do this quickly by putting the pot of milk into a sink full of cool water.

4. Add buttermilk starter culture and stir the milk gently to dissolve.

5. Pour product into quart jar and cover loosely.

6. Allow to ripen at room temperature for 16 to 18 hours.

7. After the ripening process, you will notice the milk has gotten much thicker. If you added the dry milk, the milk (now buttermilk) has become the consistency of yogurt.

8. Refrigerate for up to two weeks.

Reculturing Buttermilk from Cultured Buttermilk

As mentioned earlier, buttermilk is a serial culture. Once you have cultured an amount of buttermilk, you can keep it going indefinitely. To reculture buttermilk:

1. Warm a quart of milk to 86°.
2. Whisk in ¾ cup cultured buttermilk.
3. Allow to ripen at room temperature for about 12 hours.
4. Refrigerate.

"Quick" Buttermilk

This method of making buttermilk (not "real" buttermilk or truly cultured buttermilk) has been used by cooks for generations. This "quick" buttermilk is good if you need a fast batch of buttermilk to cook with and do not have any cultured buttermilk on hand.

Ingredients
1 pint whole milk
2 tbsp lemon juice (You can substitute 4 tbsp cream of tartar or 2 tbsp white vinegar)

Directions

1. Mix milk and lemon juice in a large, stainless-steel or glass bowl.
2. Let mixture stand at room temperature for 15 minutes.
3. Stir well before using.
4. If you do not intend on using the mixture immediately, you can keep it in a jar with a tight lid in the refrigerator for up to two weeks.

Lemon Cheese

This is a recipe that is very similar in nature to the "quick" buttermilk recipe, with a couple of extra easy steps thrown in. It will produce a delightful lemon cheese spread you can enjoy on poppy seed bagels or as a base for a great lemon cheesecake.

Ingredients

½ gallon whole milk
Approximately ¼ cup lemon juice
Coarse kosher non-iodized salt (optional)
Herbs (optional herbs might be chives, dill, or mint)

Directions

1. Directly heat the milk to 185° in a stainless steel pot.
2. Add all but 1 tbsp of the lemon juice and stir well.
3. Cover the pot and let sit for 15 to 20 minutes.
4. If curds have clearly formed, move on to the next step. If you have not yet developed a definite curd (the curds and whey have not fully separated), add the remaining lemon juice and let mixture sit another ten minutes.
5. Line a colander with a large, doubled piece of cheesecloth. Make sure the cloth is large enough that you will be able to bring the corners together in a bag for the cheese to drain.
6. Pour the curds into the cloth-lined colander to drain the whey off.
7. Tie the corners of the cloth and hang the bagged cheese to drain for about two hours.

8. Remove the cheese from the cloth and place in a glass bowl.

9. Add optional salt and herbs to taste.

10. Refrigerate in a closed container for up to two weeks.

Crème Fraiche

Another delicious dish you can make that is quite simple and will always be popular is crème fraiche, which is similar to whipped cream — only much more versatile. One of the fun things about crème fraiche is the variety of ways you can use it. You can top soups with it; use it on pancakes, bagels, and muffins; top grilled vegetables with it; or use it on fresh fruit. You will be surprised at how long its list of uses can be.

Ingredients
2 cups heavy cream
2 tbsp cultured buttermilk

Directions
1. In a double boiler, whisk cream and buttermilk together.
2. Slowly bring cream and buttermilk to about 85°.
3. Pour mixture into a glass pint jar.
4. Cover loosely and let ripen at room temperature for 12 to 24 hours or until thickened.
5. Stir and refrigerate for up to two weeks.

Mascarpone

This is a creamery product that is very similar to crème fraiche. It is commonly known as that wonderful, creamy filling that makes tiramisu.

Ingredients
1 quart light cream
¼ tsp tartaric acid (you may not need to use it all)

Directions

1. In a double boiler, heat cream to 185°.

2. Add ⅛ tsp tartaric acid and stir well to ensure it dissolves and distributes evenly throughout the mixture.

3. The mixture should begin to coagulate as the curd forms into a rice pudding-like consistency.

4. If the coagulation does not occur, add half of the remaining tartaric acid. You want to avoid adding too much tartaric acid.

5. Line a colander with a double layer of cheesecloth. Be sure the piece is big enough so when you drain the mascarpone, you will be able to tie up the corners of the cloth.

6. Use a ladle to move the curds to the cheesecloth-lined colander.

7. Drain for about an hour.

8. Place in a covered container and refrigerate for up to two weeks.

Sour Cream

Now that you have made buttermilk, you can make sour cream in a more controlled manner. Note the slight difference in ingredients between sour cream and crème fraiche. In the past, letting fresh cream sit out at room temperature was the way sour cream was made at home. The bacteria that are naturally present in the cream thickened and produced the sour taste. If you have access to farm-fresh cream, you can make sour cream in this manner.

Ingredients

2 cups light cream at room temperature
2 tbsp buttermilk at room temperature

Directions

1. Mix cream and buttermilk in a glass jar.

2. Cover tightly.

3. Allow mixture to sit at room temperature for 24 hours or until it gets thick.

4. Stir and refrigerate for 24 hours prior to use.

5. The mixture may be refrigerated for up to four weeks.

Sour Cream II

This sour cream will result in a thicker and slightly richer product than the first recipe.

Ingredients

1 cup heavy cream at room temperature
1 ¼ cups of whole milk at room temperature (not ultra-pasteurized)
½ cup cultured buttermilk at room temperature

Directions

1. Whisk the ingredients together in a stainless steel or glass bowl. Set bowl in a pan of hot water and bring the temperature of the ingredients to 80°.

2. Pour ingredients into a quart jar and cover.

3. Allow product to sit at room temperature for 16 to 24 hours until it is thick. The longer you allow it to sit at room temperature, the more sour it will become.

4. Refrigerate up to four weeks.

Quark

You may have never heard of, let alone tasted, quark. Quark is a cheese that is unknown in the United States, so you will probably not be able to find it in your supermarket.

After making quark, you will likely become a quark devotee. You will also make your first cheese, as quark is considered to be a soft cheese and involves a process you will employ in nearly every other cheese you will learn to make in this book — draining your product in a cheesecloth bag. Once you learn to make quark, you will be confident enough in your cheese making to proceed to cream cheese, yogurt cheese, cottage cheese, and more.

You can enjoy quark as you would enjoy cream cheese or yogurt. It is great on bagels, fruit, vegetables, and in cooking.

Ingredients

1 gallon pasteurized milk (You can also use a four-to-one mixture of milk and heavy cream or you can use low-fat milk, though skim is not recommended)

2 tbsp of cultured buttermilk

Directions

1. In a double boiler or in a pot of hot water, heat milk to 88°.

2. Add buttermilk and stir in gently.

3. Cover milk and let it ripen at room temperature for 24 hours. The milk will be the consistency of yogurt.

4. Line a colander with a double layer of cheesecloth. Be sure the piece is big enough so when you drain the milk, you will be able to tie up the corners of the cloth.

5. Place the colander over a large, stainless-steel pot and pour the liquid into the cloth-lined colander. You can save the liquid that pours into the pot and use it to bake with. It is great for bread.

6. Tie the corners of the cheesecloth together. The mixture in the cloth will be a sort of ball. Hang the bag to drain overnight over a bowl in your refrigerator. You can also place the bag in a colander over a bowl and place a closed container of water on top of the bag to press additional liquid out of the cheese.

7. After the mixture has drained (about eight hours), transfer it to an air-tight container and refrigerate up to two weeks.

Buttermilk Cheese

The buttermilk you used in making quark was cultured buttermilk. For this recipe, you can use the "real" buttermilk that you made when you churned cream into butter. Because there is only one necessary ingredient in this process, you can use any amount.

Ingredients

½ gallon of fresh, true buttermilk (this will yield ¾ pound of buttermilk cheese)

Salt (optional)

Directions

1. Let the buttermilk sit at room temperature for 24 hours.

2. In a stainless-steel pot, heat the buttermilk to between 160° and 180°. You will notice the curds and whey will separate as the buttermilk gets to about 160°.

3. Line a colander with a double layer of cheesecloth, making sure the cloth is large enough to tie up the corners.

4. Pour the curded buttermilk through the cheesecloth.

5. Tie the corners of the cheesecloth so you can hang the bagged curds to drain at room temperature for about four hours.

6. When the cheese has reached a consistency you desire, put it in a bowl and add salt to taste, though salt is not a necessary ingredient.

7. The cheese can be refrigerated for up to two weeks.

You will note that many of the recipes above are very similar in nature. Crème fraiche, mascarpone, cream cheese, quark, and buttermilk cheese are all very closely connected. As you become comfortable making these items, you may become adventurous and begin experimenting with different ways to make them. Other creamery items you might explore are clotted cream, cup cheese, or pashka. These are all wonderful creamery items that can be made with cream or milk.

Kefir

Kefir is a dairy product that is produced in much the same manner as buttermilk and yogurt, as it is milk cultured with a mesophilic starter. It has many health benefits because it contains beneficial bacteria and yeasts, and it is said to be the healthiest of dairy foods. In fact, the word "kefir" is believed to derive from the Turkish word "keif," which translates to "good feeling."

There are several ways to make kefir. Like buttermilk, you need to begin with a starter. You can get kefir starter as a powder or in granular form. The granular form is preferred if you would like to continue making kefir indefinitely. You can reculture kefir from the powdered form, but it has a limit of about six or seven generations. Kefir grains can be used indefinitely if you take good care of them.

If kefir is new to you, enjoy it slowly at first. Start by slowly drinking about 4 ounces a day for a couple of days and work your way up to 10 to 12 ounces over a week or two. It is a drink full of beneficial bacteria that work to help your digestive system function regularly. Do not insist on drinking a big glass quickly before you are used to it; you may experience unpleasant intestinal distress.

Kefir Made With Powdered Culture

Ingredients

1 quart of milk

½ tsp kefir powder

Directions

1. To make kefir from a powdered culture, warm a quart of milk (whole, low-fat, or skim; not ultrapasteurized) to about 90°.

2. Add ½ tsp of powder (or follow directions on package).

3. Allow to ripen at room temperature for 12 hours.

4. Refrigerate.

If you make kefir this way, you can reculture your kefir for about six or seven generations. To reculture this product, simply add 2 tbsp of your kefir to 1 quart of warm milk (80° to 90°), allow it to ripen at room temperature for eight to 12 hours, then refrigerate.

Kefir Made with Kefir Grains

Ingredients

1 quart of milk

1 to 2 tbsp kefir grains (Kefir grains are solid granules formed by lactic bacteria, yeast, protein, and lactose. These granules resemble cauliflower in their appearance)

Directions

1. Place the kefir grains into a quart jar.

2. Pour 1 quart of milk over the kefir grains.

3. Loosely cover the jar. Do not tighten the lid, as the kefir needs to breathe. A good way to cover the mixture while ripening is to cover with a triple layer of cheesecloth.

4. Allow to sit at room temperature for 12 to 72 hours. The large time variation depends on how tart you like your kefir. If you enjoy a kefir that is more tart, allow it to ripen for a longer period of time.

5. Strain the kefir into a glass jar with a non-metal strainer. This is important because metal will react with the kefir and taint it. A good choice is to use a plastic strainer.

6. Do not rinse the kefir grains in the strainer.

7. Place the grains in a jar and you are ready to make more kefir with them. The grains will last indefinitely.

If you do not plan on making another batch of kefir right away, you can simply pour a small amount of milk over the grains to moisten them and then place them in the refrigerator. If you do not make kefir for a couple of weeks, you should strain the grains and pour fresh milk over them.

You will notice as you continue to make kefir that you have a greater amount of kefir grains as they grow. Perhaps the best way to drink kefir, if you would rather not drink it on its own, is to mix it with fruit. You can simply add fresh fruit to a glass before pouring kefir, or you can use it in a smoothie.

Kefir Smoothie

Ingredients
1 frozen sliced banana
12 ounces mixed frozen berries
1 fresh sliced peach
6 to 8 ounces kefir
3 tbsp honey
3 tbsp wheat germ
8 to 12 ounces cold berry juice

Directions
1. Place all frozen fruit in a blender with the bananas at the bottom.

2. Place fresh peach on top of frozen fruit.

3. Pour kefir and berry juice over the fruit.

4. Begin blending on high.

5. As the blender is running, add honey and wheat germ.

Recipes

Take a bit of a break now from making creamery items and put a few of the items to use. Here are a few more recipes in which you can use some of the great creamery products you have already learned to make.

The list of delightful dishes that can be made with butter, sour cream, crème fraiche, mascarpone, and buttermilk is endless. Here are some familiar dishes you may have tasted but have never tried to make yourself. The recipes included here are only a sampling of the multitude of dishes you can make with some of your homemade creamery items. Included are main courses; side dishes; and bread, breakfast, and dessert dishes. Family, friends, and neighbors have tried these recipes and raved about them; yours are sure to do the same.

Alfredo sauce

This recipe utilizes heavy cream and some of the wonderful butter you made. It is simple but not for those watching their waistline. This alfredo sauce is the classic style that is traditionally served over fettuccine. You might consider adding sautéed shrimp or scallops to this as well. You can add the vegetable sauté noted earlier in this chapter as a side dish.

Ingredients
8 tbsp homemade butter
1 pint heavy cream
2 cups finely grated Parmesan cheese (You will learn to make this in Chapter 12; in several months, you can add your own homemade Parmesan to this recipe. For now, use a high-quality cheese)
1 pound pasta

Salt

Freshly ground black pepper

Directions

1. In a double boiler, melt the butter in the cream, stirring occasionally with a whisk.

2. When the cream and butter reach about 185°, whisk in the Parmesan cheese.

3. Add salt and pepper to taste.

4. Cook pasta in separate pot according to package directions until al dente (cooked, yet firm).

5. Stir pasta into sauce.

Sweet potatoes and cream

Here is a great spin on candied yams or sweet potatoes for a holiday meal. These will disappear in a flash.

Ingredients

12 large sweet potatoes, peeled and cut in chunks

1 cup homemade sour cream

¼ cup light brown sugar

1 tbsp grated, fresh ginger (You can substitute maple syrup here, or use both maple syrup and ginger)

¼ cup homemade crème fraiche

¼ cup homemade unsalted butter, melted

Salt and pepper to taste

Directions

1. In a large stock pan, boil sweet potatoes until tender.

2. Pour off water.

3. Mash potatoes using electric mixer.

4. Add crème fraiche and butter.

5. Using a large, wooden spoon, fold in sour cream, brown sugar, and ginger.

6. Salt and pepper to taste.

7. Serve immediately, or put in a casserole dish and reheat when ready to serve.

Butter pie crust

The trick to making great pies is making a flaky and tasty crust. Once you get the hang of it, you will be able to turn out incredible pies with homemade crusts filled with your favorite fruit.

Ingredients

For a single-crust pie:

1 ½ cups of unbleached all-purpose flour

½ tsp salt

½ cup (8 tbsp) unsalted butter

Cold water

For a double-crust pie:

2 cups of unbleached all-purpose flour

1 tsp salt

⅔ cup (10 ⅔ tbsp) unsalted butter

Cold water

Directions

1. Sift together flour and salt.

2. Using a pastry blender or two forks, cut the butter into the flour by quickly mixing the butter and flour together with a pastry cutter or fork. Begin by cutting in half the butter, then cut in the other half. The butter-flour mixture should be like small peas at this point.

3. Continue using the pastry blender or forks to cut in the cold water one tablespoon at a time. Each time you add water, cut it in until it is evenly distributed.

4. Add water until you can pick up a small amount of the mixture and it easily forms into a ball without crumbling.

5. Form mixture into one or two balls (depending on which recipe you used) and wrap in plastic. Refrigerate until you are ready to make the crust.

Buttermilk pancakes

These pancakes are so good that they do not require any syrup, but feel free to add the syrup anyway. For an even more irresistible treat, top them with your crème fraiche.

Ingredients

2 ½ cups unbleached all-purpose flour

½ cup whole-wheat flour

3 tbsp sugar (white or brown)

3 tsp baking powder

1 ½ tsp baking soda

¾ tsp salt

3 eggs

3 cups buttermilk

¼ cup milk (whole, low-fat, or skim)

⅓ cup (5 ⅓ tbsp) butter, melted

Directions

1. Heat a griddle or frying pan until it is hot.

2. Sift dry ingredients together.

3. Beat eggs.

4. Beat buttermilk into eggs.

5. Beat milk into wet mixture.

6. Beat melted butter into wet mixture.

7. Add wet mixture to dry mixture just before you are ready to cook.

8. Stir the two mixtures to combine them. Do not worry about lumps; they will cook out.

9. Spoon batter onto griddle or frying pan, using about 2 tbsp of batter for each pancake. You can make the pancakes larger or smaller, depending on your preference.

10. Flip the pancakes when bubbles start to appear on top.

11. Cook for about two more minutes. You can lift one to check how done the underside is.

12. Serve hot.

13. Pancakes not eaten can be frozen and reheated in the microwave. These are great for quick breakfasts.

Buttermilk oatmeal bread

This bread is a meal in itself, and works great for grilled cheese sandwiches.

Ingredients
2 cups whey
1 cup regular oatmeal (not quick-cooking oats)
4 tbsp butter
½ cup honey
1 package yeast
1 cup buttermilk
2 tsp salt
4 cups all-purpose flour
1 cup whole-wheat flour

Directions
1. Pour package of yeast into ½ cup of whey warmed to 105° to 115° in a small bowl. Allow to proof (which simply means to allow your yeast to sit

in the warm whey until it becomes active). You will notice the yeast begin to "explode" in the warm whey.

2. Bring 1 ½ cups whey to a rapid boil in a saucepan and stir in the oatmeal.

3. Once the whey is boiling again, reduce the heat and cook oats for about three minutes until it starts to thicken.

4. Remove saucepan of whey from heat, stir in the butter and honey, and pour into a large bowl.

5. When mixture has cooled to 105° to 115°, stir in the buttermilk and salt.

6. Add the yeast and beat until smooth. Be sure the mixture is no more than 115° when you add the yeast; it will kill off the yeast, and your bread will not rise.

7. Stir in 2 cups of all-purpose flour and beat until smooth.

8. Add whole-wheat flour and beat until smooth. You can use a mixer fitted with dough hooks at this point if you have one and are inclined to do so.

9. Add more flour ½ cup at a time until the dough begins to pull away from the sides of the bowl.

10. Turn the dough onto a well-floured surface and knead just until the dough is no longer sticky.

11. Knead well until the dough becomes pliable and elastic. Add flour to the surface you are working on as necessary.

12. Spread butter over the inner surface of a large bowl and put the dough in it. Be sure the bowl is large enough to allow the dough to grow to twice its size. Turn the dough to cover the surface with the butter and cover the bowl.

13. Put the bowl in a warm place (room temperature) and allow to rise until doubled in bulk.

14. Punch down and remove the dough to the lightly floured surface.

15. Knead for about one minute.

16. Divide in half and form two equal loaves.

17. Butter two regular bread pans (about 9 by 4 by 3 inches) and put a loaf in each.

18. Cover with a towel and allow the loaves to rise until about 1 inch over the top of the pans.

19. While the bread is rising, preheat your oven to 375°.

20. Put the pans into oven and bake for 40 to 45 minutes.

    a. Check brownness about 25 minutes into the baking. How brown or dark you want your bread to be is a personal preference. If you would like to slow the browning of the bread, you can cover the loaves with aluminum foil.

21. To test the bread, remove a loaf from the pan and tap on the bottom of it. The loaf should sound hollow when you tap on it.

22. Let the bread cool before slicing.

Mascarpone cheesecake

There are many variations of cheesecake that you can make with the cheese and butter recipes included in this book. When you are done learning and experimenting with all of the recipes included here, you may be able to come up with your own varieties.

Ingredients

For the crust:

1 cup slivered almonds, lightly toasted

⅔ cup chocolate wafer crumbs (These are the thin, round chocolate wafers; you can also use a graham cracker or ginger snap crust)

3 tbsp granulated white sugar

1 tbsp homemade unsalted butter, melted

For the filling:

16 ounces cream cheese at room temperature (You can buy it, or you can jump ahead to Chapter 11 and make your own, as long as you will be using your homemade mascarpone)

16 ounces homemade mascarpone at room temperature

1 ¼ cups granulated white sugar

2 tsp fresh lemon juice

1 tsp lemon zest

1 tsp pure vanilla extract

4 large eggs, room temperature

For the garnish:

Mixed berries (raspberries, blueberries, and blackberries)

Directions

To make the crust:

1. Preheat oven to 350°.

2. Butter a 9-inch springform pan and set aside.

3. Finely grind the almonds, chocolate wafer crumbs, and sugar in a food processor.

4. Add the melted butter to the almond/wafer/sugar mixture and process until moist crumbs form.

5. Press the almond/wafer/sugar mixture onto the bottom of the prepared pan (but not on the sides).

6. Bake the crust until it is set and beginning to brown, which should take about 12 minutes.

7. Remove the crust from the oven to a wire rack to cool.

8. Turn the oven temperature down to 325°.

To make the filling:

1. Beat the cream cheese, mascarpone cheese, and sugar in a large bowl just until it is smooth. Do not overbeat, or your cake will be stiff and dry.

2. Add the lemon juice and vanilla to the cream cheese/mascarpone/sugar mixture and beat until just incorporated.

3. Add the eggs to the cream cheese/mascarpone/sugar mixture one at a time, beating just until blended after each addition.

4. Pour the cheese mixture over the cooled crust.

5. Place the springform pan on an insulated cookie sheet.

6. Bake about one hour, or until the middle of the cheesecake moves slightly when the pan is gently shaken.

7. Remove the cake to a wire rack; cool for one hour or until the cake is cool to the touch.

8. Cover and refrigerate until the cheesecake is cold, at least eight hours or overnight.

9. Serve in slices with a small pool of raspberry sauce and a few berries on the side.

CASE STUDY: FONS SMITS

Traders Point Creamery
www.tpforganics.com

"I grew up in a village in the province of Friesland in the northern part of the Netherlands, surrounded by dairy farms. I studied food science and specialized in dairy science. For the past 16 years, I worked in the dairy industry around the world. I have done everything from setting up dairy coops and factories in Tanzania to assisting factories in other African and Asian countries. I worked at Cowgirl Creamery in California and developed some great cheeses for them, like the Mt. Tam. I worked for a Dutch international dairy consultancy company and started with Traders Point Creamery in 2003. At Traders Point, I started the creamery production and developed a unique product line for them in unique packaging," said Fons Smits.

"I enjoy making cheese and creamery items both commercially and as a hobby. It is my profession; however, I love the work. I like to create new things, and I like to surprise people and show them how dairy products can taste, and change their opinions."

Because Smits grew up in the Netherlands, he grew up eating Gouda; his favorite kind is the Old Amsterdam. His favorite cheese made in the United States is the Mt. Tam, and not just because he helped make it. He said when the cheese is aged right, the consistency is as soft as butter but not runny.

Smits said the hardest thing about making cheese is that you have to be patient. However, he said the more you work at making cheese, the better you will get. Although people can learn from books, more can be learned from having the curds in your hands.

"Words of wisdom to those who are just getting started in making cheese are to take your time. Also, make sure you have the setup right. Do not think every recipe will work. If you find a recipe, it is more than likely that it needs to be adjusted to your working conditions, including the milk. Keep good records because many times you can only evaluate the product after several weeks, and to make the link of a defect to how it is made is difficult without a record. If possible, ask if you can work with a cheese maker for a couple times before starting yourself."

PART THREE

Yogurt

Learning about butter was a good place to begin the process of learning about how to work with dairy products. As you work your way toward the complex process of making cheese, the next step to take is to learn to make yogurt. In this part of the book, you will learn about yogurt, its history, and how to make it.

CHAPTER 6

The Food of the Gods

Yogurt has been a great source of nutrition for 6,000 to 10,000 years. It is believed yogurt was first derived as a way to preserve milk. The milk preserved was not the cow's milk we are most familiar with today, but probably goat's or camel's milk. The word yogurt is of Turkish origin. The Assyrian word for yogurt, "lebeny," means "for life."

Nobody knows when and how yogurt was first developed, but its legend is very similar to that of butter. Many believe milk was put into a goatskin sack and tied onto the back of a camel in preparation for a journey across the desert. The heat, combined with the natural bacteria in the milk, the bacteria in the bag (which was probably made from the stomach of a goat), and the agitation of the movement of the camel aided in the fermentation of the milk. After a certain period of time, the milk ripened and developed into a custard-like substance.

There is another interesting legend about yogurt. This legend says some unhappy villagers attempted to take the life of their conqueror, Genghis Khan, by sending him some soured milk in a gourd. As the milk was being transported to the warlord, it curdled and turned into yogurt. When Khan consumed the yogurt, he was refreshed and fortified, and he continued his conquest. Whether this story of Khan is true remains unknown. It is known, though, that Khan's armies did live on yogurt; written records prove it. In the 13th century, yogurt was a main form of sustenance throughout central Asia.

Stand in the dairy aisle of your local supermarket today and you may guess that yogurt is a main form of sustenance in America today. However, the yogurt currently available in supermarkets is not the same yogurt that Genghis Khan's armies ate. Unless you are in a health food store, you may not be looking at real yogurt. What you are looking at in the dairy case of your grocery store can call itself yogurt, but before *you* call it yogurt, you have to know what yogurt truly is.

The yogurt of Khan was milk-ripened by time, temperature, and bacterial culture. The bacteria may have been different from the bacteria of today's simple plain yogurts, but you can assume there was no more to Khan's yogurt than milk and bacteria.

Pick up one of the national brands that are marketed specifically to children and you will see this list of ingredients: *Cultured pasteurized grade A milk, sugar, nonfat milk, high fructose corn syrup, modified corn starch, kosher gelatin, tri-calcium phosphate, potassium sorbate (to maintain freshness), carrageenan, natural and artificial flavors, and carmine coloring.*

Now you might be inspired to take a walk over to the organic foods section to read the ingredients on some simpler fare. Whether you are in the organic foods section of a large grocery store or in a health food store, your choice of simple, unadulterated yogurt is much smaller than your choice of sugar-filled, flavored yogurts in the main dairy case.

After you look at the variety of yogurts available to you, look at the price and compare it to the price of the yogurt product you looked at earlier. It is interesting how a product with considerably fewer ingredients can cost so much more.

All of this discussion about yogurt ingredients and price is to let you know that you can simply make yogurt — the yogurt that fortified Genghis Khan — cheaper, without unnecessary ingredients, at home.

The yogurt you make at home will have this ingredient list: milk (you can use any kind of milk as long as it is not ultra-pasteurized) and active yogurt cultures. Of course, your yogurt might also have blueberries, raspberries, strawberries, or whatever else you choose. The yogurt you make at home will only cost you what milk costs after you make your first batch of yogurt. Yogurt is a serial culture; once you make a batch, you can be set for life.

When you decide to make your own yogurt, you must then decide how to go about it and what kind of yogurt to make because there are different kinds of cultures. *Read more about the process in Chapter 7.* You can choose to take the easy route and start your yogurt simply by buying one of the unadulterated yogurts you find in the health food store, which is one that has only milk and the active cultures in it. When you do that, your resulting yogurt will comprise a yogurt with the cultures listed on the container you used as a starter.

If you purchase a starter that has *S. thermophilus, L. acidophilus, bifidus,* and *L. bulgaris,* your resulting yogurt will contain those cultures and be of a similar nature to the original culture. You may, however, choose to start from a starter you order from a dairy supply source. By doing this, you may be able to be a little more specific as to the nature of the yogurt you culture.

You might enjoy your yogurt very thick, or you might like it to be a thin, drinkable yogurt. Some yogurt cultures are "countertop" cultures, meaning you are able to ripen them without the use of heat beyond room temperature. Some yogurts require heat of about 110° for eight hours. Other yogurts are extremely tart, while some are very mild. There are yogurts that are better made with cream or whole milk, while some are good with skim milk. *You will find resources to begin your yogurt quest in the back of this book.*

You might enjoy a particular kind of yogurt, or you may want to have several varieties available to use in different ways. Because the only cost in yogurt making, once you make your original batch, is in the cost of the milk or cream, you will be able to have a whole refrigerator full of simple yogurt you made that will continue to culture for years to come.

CHAPTER 7

How to Make Yogurt

I f you go back to the previous chapter and remember the legend of Genghis Khan, you might think you can put milk into a gourd, walk around with it on a warm Mongolian plain, and you will have yogurt. Although yogurt is relatively simple to make, you do need to understand a few basic principles involved in consistently producing yogurt that you will not be afraid to eat or feed your family. You are not going to kill anyone by giving them curdled sour milk, but you may turn up a few noses.

Yogurt is fermented milk. The fermentation occurs when a starter culture of *Lactobacillus bulgaricus, Lactobacillus acidophilus,* and *Streptococcus thermophilus* are introduced to milk. Some yogurts contain only two of these cultures, and some contain all three. The culture produces lactic acid during the fermentation of lactose, a sugar found in milk.

There are various types of yogurt cultures that will produce different tastes and consistencies of yogurt:

- **Filmjölk culture** produces a medium-thick yogurt with tart flavor much like buttermilk
- **Matsoni culture** makes a very thick yogurt that is extremely tart

- **Piimä culture** will make a thin, drinkable yogurt that is quite mild
- **Viili culture** will make a thick yogurt with a relatively mild flavor

The basic steps you will take in making yogurt are to heat milk to a temperature that will kill off any microorganisms that may exist in the milk (about 185°). The microorganisms might compete with the bacteria you will introduce into the milk that will turn the milk to yogurt. After you introduce the yogurt culture, you will hold the mixture at such a temperature that will encourage the growth of the beneficial bacterium (about 110°).

Like making butter, making yogurt it is a simple process. It is slightly more time-consuming than butter, but once you get it down, you will be able to get it started quickly and easily produce yogurt. The most challenging step in the process of making yogurt is holding the yogurt at 110° for six to eight hours while it ripens. There are numerous ways you can do this, some more successful than others. *Various methods of accomplishing this will be discussed within this chapter.*

If you find you enjoy making and eating homemade yogurt, you might consider purchasing a yogurt maker. You can buy yogurt makers that make yogurt in little serving-sized cups, or you can buy a yogurt maker that makes yogurt in a large vat. You can spend as little as $30 or as much as $500 on a yogurt maker, but you can usually get a fairly good home yogurt maker for $60 to $80. Yogurt makers give you a very controlled way of maintaining the ideal temperature needed to make yogurt. Yogurt makers vary in style and features, but the primary function of a yogurt maker is to keep the yogurt at a consistent temperature for an extended (six to eight hours) period of time. *You will find suggestions for locations to purchase yogurt makers in the Appendix of this book.*

If you do not have a yogurt maker, try a few of the methods suggested here. See how easy it is and how much you enjoy making and eating homemade yogurt. If you enjoy eating the yogurt but find the methods here too cumbersome, shop for a yogurt maker that will operate in a manner that fits your lifestyle. You can think about yogurt makers in the same way that people think about bread machines: Some people like engaging in the process of mixing and kneading the dough as much as they enjoy the taste of homemade bread, while others enjoy the fresh bread but have neither the time nor patience to get involved in the particulars.

Regardless of whether you decide to buy a yogurt maker, once you begin to make your own yogurt, you will save money over buying it at the store. Once you make your first batch, the only cost to you will be milk — and a gallon of milk is less expensive than a gallon of yogurt. Even if you will be making your yogurt from organic milk, you will still save money.

Basic Yogurt

Ingredients

Milk (Whole, low-fat, or skim may be used. You may also use dry milk by following the package directions on reconstituting. Do not use ultra-pasteurized milk)

Active yogurt culture (You may use live cultures that you purchase from a health food store or cheese supply store. You may also use yogurt that has live active cultures; check the label to be sure. Also, when using yogurt, be sure it is the freshest available, with no additives. If you cannot find a yogurt that does not include pectin, you are probably all right with the pectin. Pectin is a natural, plant-based thickening agent. If you use yogurt to culture the yogurt you are making, use ¼ cup per quart of milk)

Instant nonfat dry milk (This is optional. If you like your yogurt a little thicker, you can use ¼ to ½ cup dry milk)

Directions

1. In a double boiler, heat milk to 185°. Stir frequently.

2. After milk reaches 185°, cool to 105° to 122°. The ideal temperature for your ripening yogurt is 122°. A temperature above 130° will kill the culture.

3. Stir yogurt culture into milk.

4. Transfer mixture to a sterilized glass jar that can be fitted with a tight cap.

5. Maintain temperature between 105° & 122° for six to eight hours.

6. Refrigerate.

The question now becomes: How do you hold the temperature for six to eight hours if you do not have a yogurt maker?

1. If you have a slow cooker with a "warm" setting, you can fill it with water and set your jars of yogurt in the slow cooker. Be sure to keep a close eye on the temperature of the water.

2. You can fill a cooler with warm water and place your jars of yogurt in the water at the preferred temperature. Make sure the cooler stays closed for the required time to incubate. You can provide additional insulation by placing a towel over the cooler.

3. You can wrap the jar(s) in a personal heating pad. Again, check the temperature of the pad to make sure it does not get too hot.

4. You can pour the yogurt into a thermos. The best kind of thermos for this operation is one with a wide mouth; a small-mouth thermos can be problematic when it comes to removing thickened yogurt.

5. Preheat your oven to 150° or its lowest possible setting, then turn it off. Use an oven thermometer to monitor its temperature. Place your yogurt in the oven after it has reached 120°. You can turn your oven on and off to keep it at the ideal temperature. Watch it closely.

6. If you have a home appliance that runs hot or produces a good deal of heat, you can wrap your jar of yogurt in a towel and place it on the appliance. People have been known to incubate their yogurt on televisions, personal computers, and audio equipment. This works but it is not recommended.

7. If you live in a warm climate, you can simply wrap your jar of yogurt in a towel and put it in a warm part of the house.

As you can see, as long as you do not let your yogurt go below 98°or over 130°, it is a pretty good bet that once you incubate the milk, you will end up with yogurt. If you do let the temperature fall below 98°, do not worry. You have not ruined your yogurt, and it will still ripen once you get the temperature up. The taste may be a little more tart, but you will still get yogurt.

If, on the other hand, your mixture gets too hot, you have destroyed the culture, and you will have to start over again.

Troubleshooting Yogurt

If your yogurt is too thin after six to eight hours of incubation:

- You may have allowed your milk to cool too much before you added your starter. Try to add starter when the milk temperature is between 105° and 120°.

- You may not have kept your yogurt warm enough during the six to eight-hour incubation period. Remember, yogurt will not ripen at temperatures below 98°.

- If you used farm-fresh milk, there may have been antibiotics present in the milk that killed the starter. If you use farm-fresh milk, let it sit in your refrigerator for at least 48 hours before you use it to make yogurt.

- You may have used a weak starter. If you use yogurt as a starter, make sure it is as fresh as possible. If you use store-bought yogurt, check the expiration date. Also, it is good to date the yogurt you make and keep in your refrigerator so you know that you are always using the freshest possible starter.

- You may not have properly rinsed your equipment before making yogurt. Detergent can have an ill effect on the starter, not to mention give it a bad taste.

If you have curdled yogurt after the six- to eight-hour incubation period:

- You may have heated the milk too high before adding your starter.

- Your milk may have been too hot when you added your starter.

If your yogurt has a bad taste:

- You may have scorched the milk while heating it. If you do not use a double boiler, be sure that you constantly stir the milk and monitor its temperature.

- The jars or containers that you incubate your yogurt in may not have been clean. It is vital that everything is clean and free of detergent.

You may have allowed your yogurt to incubate too long. The long incubation period will give your yogurt a tart flavor. Six to eight hours is usually a long enough period to incubate yogurt.

- Your milk, milk powder, or starter may have been spoiled. Make sure everything you use is fresh.

Now that you have succeeded in making plain yogurt, you probably would like to enjoy flavored yogurt. There are a number of ways to go about flavoring your yogurt.

If you enjoy vanilla yogurt, you can add a drop or two of vanilla extract to the milk when you add the starter. The amount of vanilla extract you add will be determined by the type of vanilla you use and how much you like vanilla. You can flavor your yogurt in a similar manner with any one of a number of flavor extracts, including coffee extract, honey, maple syrup, or chocolate syrup.

For fruit-flavored yogurt, the easiest thing to do this is add fresh fruit to your yogurt just before you eat it. If fresh fruit is not an option, try frozen fruit. You might also choose to add a fruit preserve or jam to your yogurt.

Once you get used to the process of making your own yogurt, you may want to keep it going and have fresh or frozen yogurt every day. *There are a couple of recipes for frozen yogurt later on in Chapter 8.* Other than frozen yogurt goodies you might make, you will probably want to store yogurt in your refrigerator for no more than a week. Make sure the yogurt is stored in an airtight container.

CHAPTER 8

Beyond Basic Yogurt

Yogurt could well be the most versatile food in your refrigerator. When you start to make your own yogurt, you will discover more things you can do with it. In this chapter, you will find a number of recipes that cover every meal of the day — and just about every course of every meal. The goal here is to give you a beginning for your uses of yogurt. Some of the recipes are basic recipes that you can even improvise on. Have fun and be creative.

Recipes with Yogurt

Yogurt cheese

One of the most wonderful aspects about yogurt is it takes on the flavor of just about anything you mix with it. This yogurt cheese can be mixed with many items, from chocolate to peanut butter to hot salsa. It is easy to make and has endless possibilities.

Ingredients
Yogurt (Let the amount you need govern the amount of yogurt you start with. One quart of yogurt will yield 1 ½ cups of yogurt cheese)
Salt (optional)

Directions

1. Place a doubled piece of cheesecloth in a colander. Be sure the piece is big enough so when you drain the yogurt, you will be able to tie up the corners of the cloth.

2. Pour the yogurt into the cheesecloth.

3. Allow yogurt to drain into a bowl for 30 minutes. Save the whey to bake with.

4. Tie up corners of cheesecloth and hang over a bowl in the refrigerator for 12 to 24 hours. How long you let it drain will determine the consistency of your cheese. The longer you allow the yogurt to drain, the firmer your cheese will be.

5. Put the drained yogurt cheese into a bowl and mix in salt, if you choose to add it.

6. It will store for one week in a tightly sealed bowl in the refrigerator.

Yogurt biscuits

Here is a very easy and basic recipe that employs yogurt as a "wet" ingredient in a baked item. If you have never used yogurt in place of milk in recipes that call for milk, give this one a try. Once you make this, you can use this recipe as a base from which to experiment further.

Ingredients

3 cups white flour (You can also choose to use 1 ½ cups white flour and 1 ½ cups wheat flour)

2 level tsp of baking powder

2 level tsp baking soda

½ tsp salt

6 tbsp cold unsalted butter (You can choose to use 3 tbsp butter and 3 tbsp canola oil)

3 tbsp packed brown sugar (optional)

One or two eggs (room temperature)

1 ¼ cup firm yogurt (If your yogurt is runny, drain it through some cheesecloth for about 15 to 20 minutes)

½ cup raisins, dates, dried cherries, chocolate chips, or any other add-ins that you might want

Directions

1. Preheat oven to 400°.

2. Lightly butter a baking sheet.

3. Sift together the flour, baking powder, baking soda, and salt.

4. Add butter and brown sugar.

5. With a pastry cutter, cut butter and brown sugar into the dry ingredients.

6. If you are using the canola oil, cut it in after you cut in the butter and brown sugar.

7. You can choose to cut the dry ingredients together with the butter, brown sugar, and canola oil using a food processor fitted with a stainless-steel blade.

8. In a small bowl, beat together the yogurt and one egg.

9. Make a well in the center of the dry ingredients and lightly mix in the yogurt/egg mixture and any add-ins (raisins, nuts, etc.) you may have. Do not over-mix; mix only till blended.

10. Drop by ¼ cup amounts onto the buttered baking sheet.

11. Beat the other egg and brush the dropped biscuits with the egg mixture.

12. Bake about 15 minutes. Peek at them at about 12 or 13 minutes.

13. Serve warm with butter, crème fraiche, and/or jam.

Tzatziki

(pronounced za ZEE kee)

This is a great dip of Greek origin for vegetables, pita, or pita chips. The cucumber gives it a refreshing taste, while the garlic gives it a bit of a bite. It is wonderful as a topping on falafel sandwiches.

Ingredients

4 cups fresh, homemade plain yogurt (Whole-milk yogurt is preferred here. Also, you may prefer a yogurt that is more tart than yogurt you would enjoy eating plain or with fruit. If you make yogurt specifically for this recipe, try to let it incubate for eight hours)

One medium-sized, peeled, and coarsely grated cucumber

4 crushed garlic cloves

2 tbsp olive oil

½ tsp dried dill

Salt

Freshly ground black pepper

Directions

1. Place a doubled piece of cheesecloth in a colander. Be sure the piece is big enough so when you drain the yogurt, you will be able to tie up the corners of the cloth.

2. Drain the yogurt into a bowl for about two hours. Retain the whey to use for baking.

3. Place the grated cucumber in a colander and allow to drain for the same amount of time that you drain the yogurt.

4. After the yogurt and the cucumber have drained, mix them together with the garlic, olive oil, and dill.

5. Add salt and pepper to taste.

Pineapple frappé (smoothie)

This version makes a great breakfast or lunch. It is great with other dishes or as a meal itself.

Ingredients

1 frozen banana

2 to 3 cups of frozen pineapple chunks

2 cups of chilled pineapple or orange juice (or a combination of the two)

3 tbsp honey

1 cup of homemade yogurt

Directions

1. Place bananas, pineapple, and juice in blender.

2. Blend on high.

3. As blender is running, add yogurt and honey.

4. Serve immediately.

Frozen Yogurt

Making frozen yogurt initially seems to be a simple matter: make yogurt and stick it in the freezer. You probably flavor it with vanilla or strawberries and wait several hours before you take it out of the freezer and you have a frozen gelatinous treat. There are a few tricks to making frozen yogurt. Here you will find directions on making great-tasting frozen yogurt with and without an ice cream maker.

One of the primary difficulties that you may run across in making frozen yogurt is the yogurt you use has too much liquid in it. If you look in various recipe books for directions on making frozen yogurt, many of them will call for "Greek-style yogurt." Greek-style yogurt is somewhat thicker than your standard supermarket American brands of yogurt and has a slightly tangier flavor to it. In making frozen yogurt, it is not the tangy flavor you are looking for, but the thickness. If you attempt to make frozen yogurt with a yogurt that is even a little runny, you will not be happy with the results. How tangy you want the yogurt you will use to make frozen yogurt will depend on your tastes and what flavor of frozen yogurt you will be making. Some flavors (chocolate, for example) are better suited to the tang than others (such as vanilla).

If you are making yogurt with the intent of making frozen yogurt, you will start by adding instant nonfat dry milk to your milk, especially if you are making your yogurt with low-fat or skim milk. Add a ¼ cup of instant nonfat dry milk for each quart of milk you use to make yogurt. The solids you are adding to the milk will help to make your yogurt thick and creamy. If you would like your yogurt to have less tang, let it ripen for only six hours. You may even want to check your yogurt after five hours. If you want your yogurt to be tangier, let it ripen for eight hours.

Before you proceed with making frozen yogurt with your homemade yogurt, be sure that your yogurt has not curdled at all. If your yogurt has a lumpy appearance, it may have curdled. You want to start with the smoothest, creamiest yogurt possible.

If your yogurt shows signs of being even slightly runny, drain it in a colander lined with a double layer of cheesecloth for about 15 minutes. You now will have a thick, creamy, Greek-style yogurt necessary to make great frozen yogurt.

Making Frozen Yogurt without an Ice Cream Maker

Like the last recipe, you can adapt this using just about any ingredients you desire. Again, the trick here is to keep the yogurt cold and moving around regularly. This recipe is being written at the height of peach season, which is why a peach-flavored frozen yogurt was made.

Ingredients
3 cups homemade yogurt
1 cup cream (you might substitute whole milk)
¾ cup white sugar
4 peeled and sliced peaches
⅛ tsp salt

Directions
1. Place all ingredients into a blender and blend until smooth.
2. Place mixture into a freezer-safe bowl.
3. Place bowl in freezer.
4. Allow to freeze for 45 minutes.
5. Remove from freezer and whisk mixture.
6. Return to freezer for 30 minutes.

7. Remove from freezer and whisk mixture.

8. Return to freezer for 30 minutes.

9. Remove from freezer and whisk mixture.

10. The yogurt should be well-set at this point. If you do not plan on eating it immediately, you can allow it to freeze. If you would like it to be a little softer when you eat it, you can microwave it for about 30 seconds.

Making Frozen Yogurt with an Ice Cream Maker

Ice cream makers keep the mixture that you place inside them cold as they keep the mixture moving. The cold temperature and the motion allow the mixture to freeze without becoming frozen solid. The following recipe is for a simple vanilla yogurt. You may add any ingredients you desire at the first stage of this recipe. If you are making chocolate frozen yogurt, you can add a good-quality chocolate syrup at the first stage. You may also want to try adding sliced fruit or chocolate chips. If you are making a fruit-flavored yogurt, try running the fruit through a food processor before adding it. Remember, you want to keep the liquid level to a minimum. If you add processed fruit, it is important that your yogurt is thick. If you do not care how rich your frozen yogurt is (that is, how high the fat content), you can add about 6 tbsp of crème fraiche to the following recipe.

Ingredients
3 cups homemade yogurt
¾ cup white sugar
1 tsp pure vanilla extract

Directions
1. In a large bowl, whisk together all ingredients until sugar is completely dissolved.

2. Cover bowl with plastic wrap and refrigerate for two to three hours.

3. Place mixture in ice cream maker and operate according to manufacturer's directions.

4. Place mixture in freezer if you do not plan to eat it immediately.

The recipes above serve to demonstrate just how versatile yogurt is. You can use yogurt to dress salads, in soup stock to make creamy soups, in main dishes (try a good tangy yogurt on a chicken paprikash rather than a high-fat sour cream), and, of course, in many desserts (try making a Waldorf salad — a fruit and walnut salad tossed in mayonnaise — using yogurt in place of the traditional mayo; the salad is not as rich as the mayo variety and has far fewer calories). Be guided by your creativity, and you will find no end to the uses of yogurt.

CASE STUDY: CATHA LINK

Alpine Lakes Sheep Cheese

Catha Link makes the cheese at Alpine Lakes Sheep Cheese. She has been making cheese commercially for seven years and said she enjoys making cheese because there are so many different varieties.

"It would take a lifetime to try everything, and I never get tired of it," Link said. "The hardest thing about making cheese is the time it takes. Waiting for the cheese to age so that you can taste it takes a great deal of patience."

She said, "I love to make soft-ripened cheeses because after a couple of days, the bloom magically appears. My favorite cheese to eat depends on the time of the year, but I like sharp, aged cheeses and soft-ripened cheeses.

"A word of advice to those who are just getting started in making cheese is that if the bacteria makeup of your cheese is sound, never throw any of it away. Even if you didn't end up making what you wanted, you can usually make it into some kind of cheeses that is good to eat. Be creative with it."

PART FOUR

Cheese

You have already made several simple and very basic cheeses. Buttermilk cheese, yogurt cheese, and quark are good beginnings to understanding the basics of cheese making. This part of the book will begin by looking at the history and world of cheese. The following chapters will then describe how to make cheese, beginning with the simple recipes and progressing to the more complex and time-consuming recipes.

CHAPTER 9

So Much Cheese, So Many Stories

There are between 400 and 2,000 kinds of cheese in the world. It is difficult to establish a precise number because it depends on how you define the great variety of cheese types. Cheese is thought to have been a part of the human diet for more than 4,000 years.

To tell the story of how cheese was first "discovered" would be to tell a tale similar to how butter and yogurt were discovered: The desert traveler filled a saddlebag from the stomach of an animal with milk, and the natural contents of the stomach, combined with the heat and the agitation of the ride, turned the milk into curds and whey.

That is the short story; beyond that, the story gets very complicated and changes from place to place. Because there are so many different kinds of cheese in the world, there are equally as many stories as to how each of them developed.

The development of a particular kind of cheese was determined by geography, agriculture, types of domesticated animals, climate, and a number of other factors.

In some locations, goats are the prevalent source of milk for cheese, while in other locations, the milk comes from cows, sheep, camel, yak, or buffalo. What the animals eat is also a factor that determines types and taste of various cheeses. Explore cheese made in the United States today; you will come across cheese makers who boast grass-fed cows as opposed to cows that are fed a diet of corn. Another factor that affects cheese is whether the cow has eaten grass in the spring, summer, or fall because seasonal variations in diet affect the flavor of the cheese made from the milk of naturally feeding livestock.

How the animal milk is processed is another element that plays into the making of cheese. Cheese connoisseurs will tell you that "good" cheese cannot be made with commercially pasteurized milk because this process kills off many of the organisms that contribute to the flavor of cheese made with raw milk.

Where and how a cheese is aged also contributes to its flavor. Aged cheese is traditionally kept in places known as caves for months at a time. Sometimes caves are just large refrigerators that control the temperature and humidity, allowing the cheese to mature in a perfectly balanced environment. However, today some cheeses are still aged in actual caves.

The best example of the cheese cave is the Roquefort cheese cave in the south of France. Roquefort cheese is made from unpasteurized ewe's milk and is then aged in huge natural caves found only in that particular area of southern France. In the olden days, an interesting thing happened to the cheese during the aging process: A mold that is native to the soils in the cave grew on the ewe's milk cheese, giving the cheese a very strong and distinct flavor. As cheese makers experimented with this mold and their processes developed, they began growing the mold on bread to better control its inoculation into the cheese. Today, the mold is grown in laboratories, but the cheese is still aged in those same natural caves. Only cheese that is made in this specific area of southern France and aged in those caves can be truly called Roquefort cheese.

On the other end of the cheese spectrum from Roquefort cheese is what we all know as American cheese, which is a product of American industrialization. However, American cheese shares at least one thing with Roquefort: you cannot make it at home.

James Kraft developed American cheese in the beginning of the 20th century. The cheese was developed using milk that was pasteurized in such a way that all bacteria and mold were killed, and the cheese was guaranteed not to spoil. For many years, the cheese was canned. Kraft patented his cheese in 1916, and more than half the cheese sold in the United States today is American cheese.

According to the Midwest Dairy Association, the most popular natural cheese sold in the United States is cheddar. Cheddar occupies a comfortable middle ground between Roquefort and American cheese and is a kind of cheese that you can make at home.

Cheddar cheese was named for a region in much the same way that Roquefort was. Cheddar cheese was developed in the West Country of England in the 12th century. The cheese developed its specific flavor due to the diet the local cows grazed on and the Cheddar Caves where the cheese was aged. Cheddar has become a very popular cheese worldwide for a couple of different reasons. Cheddar cheese has a wonderful flavor that is complex but not overpowering. Also, because it is a hard cheese, it is low in water content, giving it a longer shelf life.

Cheddar cheese has suffered the same way that cheese has suffered as a food at the hands of American industrialization. As you look at a consumer's choice of cheddar cheese, you will see that you can purchase what is known as "American cheddar," or you can purchase true natural cheddar. American cheddar is not labeled as such, but the term "American" refers to the industrial mass production used to manufacture a product similar to the way American cheese is manufactured.

Natural cheddar does not have to be made in Somerset, England, like Roquefort has to be made in the caves in the south of France; you can get wonderful American-made cheddars that are made by hand by artisan cheese makers. However, true cheddar hails from one of four counties in England (Somerset, Dorset, Devon, or Cornwall) and is made from the local milk of the cows that eat the local vegetation.

Artisans

An artisan is a skilled individual who studies and practices a particular craft and/or trade. Artisan cheese makers practice the age-old art of making cheese in small batches by hand. Though this book is concerned with making cheese and other creamery products, the term "artisan" is also applied to bakers, brewers, furniture makers, wine makers, and skilled workers in many different fields.

There are stories for each and every cheese you might find in your supermarket, delicatessen, or neighborhood cheese shop. Each story tells a particular geographic and cultural history specific to the type of cheese it refers to. As you learn about each of the cheeses described in the coming chapters, you will read a little history of the cheese you will be learning to make. You will see that in many cases, the history has a direct relation to how the cheese is made, so the history is as much a part of the process of making the cheese as anything else.

Great Facts about Cheese

- Americans consume nearly 9 billion pounds of cheese each year. That means that the average individual consumes approximately 31 pounds of cheese each year.

- Americans spend nearly $40 billion on cheese every year.

- Mozzarella cheese rivals cheddar for the favorite cheese of choice by the American consumer with about 3 billion pounds of each cheese being eaten every year.

- Wisconsin is the top cheese-producing state in the United States, with California a close second and catching up fast.

- The most popular recipe that includes cheese in the United States is macaroni and cheese.

- What appears to be the remains of 4,000-year-old cheese have been found in Egyptian tombs.

- The term "The Big Cheese" is a reference to Thomas Jefferson, who ordered and had delivered a block of cheese that weighed more than 1,000 pounds to Monticello in 1800.

- The word "cheese" is a distant relative of the Latin word "caseus." The Anglo-Saxon derivation of the word is "cese," which became the English "cheese."

- Mark your calendar for:
  - National Grilled Cheese Sandwich Month in April
  - National Cheese Fondue Day on April 11
  - National Cheeseball Day on April 17
  - National Cheese Day on June 4

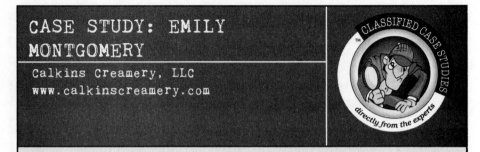

CASE STUDY: EMILY
MONTGOMERY

Calkins Creamery, LLC
www.calkinscreamery.com

Emily Montgomery is the master cheese maker at her family's farm creamery. Her family has been making cheese commercially for three years, and she and her husband have a background in the food industry.

"I enjoy learning about all of the factors that impact the final product, from the cows' diets to the climate in our aging room. The hardest thing about making cheese is that the job consists of long hours seven days per week. It seems like we're never done! My favorite cheese to make is Basket Tomme, but my favorite cheese to eat is Caerphilly-style cheese."

Montgomery advises those getting starting in the cheese-making business to start with a solid background of food safety. She also says cheese makers should not overlook distribution. While it may not be glamorous, it is very important to the process.

CHAPTER 10

How to Make Cheese

You have already made several types of very basic cheese when you prepared yogurt cheese, buttermilk cheese, and quark in earlier chapters. These are simple cheeses that are very tasty and easy to make, and they also give you a solid understanding of some of the procedures you will be involved with as you progress to the more complex operation of making soft, Italian, whey, hard, and mold- and bacteria-ripened cheeses. Each step of the different processes will be explained in precise and simple terms, and the processes will grow more complex with each type of cheese explained, with the exception of making whey cheese. The process of making whey cheese is placed later in this book because the whey used to make the several types of cheese described here is a product of cheese making itself. *See Chapter 13 for more on making whey.*

This chapter will start by breaking down the process of cheese making. In the same manner that making yogurt, buttermilk, and kefir were very similar, so too is making cheese. Each cheese has its own specific procedure, but there are some cheese-making steps that apply to nearly all of the cheeses you will make.

Heating the Milk

Whether you use farm-fresh milk or milk you have purchased at your local grocery store, you will need to heat the milk to start just about any cheese-making procedure. The temperature you heat your milk to will be determined by the type of cheese you are making and the type of bacteria culture you add to the milk.

Pasteurization involves heating milk and has been covered in Chapter 2, so that process will be left out of any recipe directions. However, there are several recipes in the following chapters that suggest you use farm-fresh milk. Be aware that if you choose to use this ingredient, you should have a good source of farm-fresh raw milk.

When you heat your milk, you may choose from one of several options: You can heat your milk directly on the stovetop in a stainless-steel pot; you can heat your milk in a double boiler; or you can heat your milk in a hot water bath.

If you choose to heat your milk directly on the stovetop, you should do so very slowly with a sharp eye on your milk, as direct heating tends to be uneven. You should stir constantly when you heat your milk directly on your stovetop burner. Direct heating is the least desirable method of heating milk for making cheese because it does not heat the milk as evenly as indirect heating does.

Indirectly heating milk in a double boiler is the suggested approach for heating milk that calls for a thermophilic starter. Thermophilic starters will usually require the milk and then the curds to be heated to 115° to as much as 145°, slowly, over extended periods of time. Indirect heating with a double boiler heats the milk evenly. Many recipes will call for you to heat your milk or curds to a specific temperature over a long period of time, and you may be required to raise the temperature of the milk by 1° or 2° every five minutes. Indirect heating with a double boiler is the best way to accomplish this.

Another way you might choose to heat your milk is by using a hot water bath in your kitchen sink, which is an easy and very controlled way to heat milk in which you will be using a mesophilic starter. Most cheese that you will make using a mesophilic starter will only require that your milk be heated to between 95° and 110°. When you heat milk in a hot water bath, you are able to control the temperature of the milk by adding hot water if your milk cools down or by removing the pot from the bath if it gets too hot.

Adding the Starter

The next step in most cheese making is adding the starter, which most of the time is done in the initial heating of the milk. *Starters were described in Chapter 2 on the various ingredients a home creamery uses.*

When you add a starter to heated milk, be sure you stir it in well to distribute the starter evenly throughout the milk.

Coagulating the Milk

After allowing the starter to sit for a short period of time (times vary depending on the type of cheese you are making), you will add the rennet, which is the substance that will help make the curd. To further aid in coagulating milk, you might also add an acid at this point of the operation. *See the definition of applicable acids in Chapter 2.*

Again, when you add a coagulating agent to the heated milk, you should gently stir with an up-and-down motion to ensure the coagulant is properly distributed. Also, to assure proper distribution, you may dilute the coagulant in ¼ cup of cool, unchlorinated water.

In most cheese-making procedures, the coagulated milk will be required to sit at a specific temperature for a specific amount of time. Sometimes you will be required to raise the temperature very slowly over a couple of hours.

Cutting the Curds

After the milk has been allowed to ripen for a time with the coagulant (again, times will vary depending on the type of cheese you are making), you will notice the milk has become a thick, custard-like consistency. You will know that the curds are ready to be cut when there is a clean break in the surface of the curd when you stick a (clean) finger into them. A clean break means that a soft crack appears in the curd's surface and your finger comes out clean. If the milk is still yogurt-like, your curds are not yet ready to be cut.

Knowing when your curds are ready to be cut takes some practice. You will know if the curds have not developed enough because they will not cut cleanly, and a clean break is not apparent when you stick your finger or a curd knife in. On the other hand, you can also wait too long before you cut them, and the result will be that the curds become too hard and mash when you try to cut them.

If you test your curds and they are not ready, wait another five minutes and try again. Keep a close eye on them.

Patience

The best advice you might get as a beginning cheese maker is to be patient. Making cheese is not a quick process. You must learn to have patience and the ability to wait until the moment is just right to perform certain operations. Sometimes that wait might be five minutes, and sometimes the wait might be five weeks or longer.

Cutting the curd is done to allow the whey to separate from the curd. Different cheeses call for different size curds to be cut. To cut the curds, follow this procedure, supposing that you are required to cut ¾-inch curds:

1. Place your curd knife into the pot at the pot's center and cut down to the bottom of the pot.

2. Draw the curd knife across the entire width of the pot, making a cut from the top of the curd to the bottom of the curd and all the way across the center of the pot. At this point, you will have cut the mass of curd in half.

3. Withdraw your curd knife and make another cut from top to bottom, ¾ inch and parallel to your first cut.

4. Go to the other side of your first cut and make a parallel cut, ¾ inch from top to bottom.

5. Continue cutting in this manner until you have a series of parallel cuts that are ¾ inch apart, covering the top of the curd.

6. Turn the pot 90° and repeat this operation. When you are done, the top of the curds will look like a checkerboard pattern of ¾-inch squares.

7. Using the previously cut squares as a guide, insert your curd knife at a 45° angle and cut along each of the top cut lines in this manner. You will be cutting the curds at a 45° angle from top to bottom. If you were to look at a bisection of your cut curds, they would appear diamond-shaped.

8. After you have cut your curds, allow them to sit for a short period of time before you stir them, allowing the curds to firm up a bit.

9. Gently use a spatula to stir the curds, bringing the bottom curds to the top.

10. Any curds that seem much larger than others should be cut.

11. It is not vital that the curds are all the same size, but they should be all be relatively similar in size so as to allow for an even drainage.

12. Allow the curds to rest for five minutes.

Cooking the Curds

Cooking curds is done to release more whey from the cut curds. Different cheese recipes will call for you to cook the curds at different temperatures for different periods of time. As you cook your curds, you should also gently stir them. Heed the word "gentle;" there is precious buttermilk in those curds that you want to retain. If you allow too much buttermilk to escape as you release the whey, the cheese will end up with an undesirable consistency.

Most cheese requires that the curds be cooked by raising the temperature very slowly over an extended period of time. The type of cheese you are making will determine the length and the temperature to which you will cook your curds.

Draining the Curds

This is the point where cheese recipes will begin to vary greatly. Standard operating procedure for many cheeses is to ladle or pour the curd very carefully into a colander lined with cheesecloth. Below is a list of some common ways to drain the whey from curds:

Draining soft cheese

Gather the corners of the cheesecloth that holds the curds, making a cloth bag for the curds that will be hung to allow the whey to drain. You can run a wooden spoon through the knot in the cheesecloth to hang your bag inside a large pot. You can also try to hang the bag from a hook over your sink.

Draining hard cheese

How you drain hard cheese varies greatly depending on what kind of cheese you are making. Directions for draining hard cheese will be given in each cheese recipe.

Draining bacteria-ripened cheese

Bacteria-ripened cheese is not pressed, but drained in an open-ended cheese mold. The cheese mold, with the curds inside it, has a cheese mat on the bottom and top, with a cheese board on the top and bottom of those. The entire operation sits in a draining pan, allowing the cheese to be flipped to allow for adequate drainage.

Remember to drain your curds over a bowl and save the expelled whey. There will be recipes later in this book for different things you can do with that whey, and you will learn about several kinds of cheese that you can make with fresh whey. If you are not able to use the whey immediately, you can refrigerate it for up to a week and then use it for baking.

Milling the Cheese

After the cheese has drained, many hard cheese recipes will call for you to break the drained curds up into smaller pieces by hand using a process called "milling." Similar to stirring the curds earlier in the cheese-making procedure, you need to mill the curds very carefully, taking care not to force any of the precious butterfat out of the curd.

Salting the Cheese

Many cheese recipes will call for salt at this point in the cheese-making process. *Cheese salt was discussed in Chapter 2.* The type of cheese you are making will determine how you add salt, and there are several ways to go about doing this.

Brining

Different types of cheese call for different levels of salt in your brine, which is a solution made of salt and water. Some cheeses will require a brine solution that is merely lightly salted water, while other cheeses will require a super-saturated brine solution.

A super-saturated brine solution is made by adding 2 pounds of cheese salt into 1 gallon of water that is just short of boiling. After the salt is added and stirred in, remove the solution from the stove to cool. Chill the solution.

You can reuse the brine several times if you boil it after each use. Because some of the salt may be lost after each use, add additional salt to the point where it no longer dissolves in the solution. This lets you know that the water is fully saturated.

If you find that your cheese dissolves in a brine solution, you may add salt directly to the curds. If your cheese dissolves during the brining process, you may have used ultra-pasteurized milk. Next time, make sure that the milk you use is not ultra-pasteurized.

Directly adding salt

For soft cheese, you will take the curds out of their cheesecloth bag, place them in a bowl, and add salt to taste. Again, stir the salt in gently.

To salt hard cheese, sprinkle the salt over the curds after you have milled them. Gently mix the salt into the curds to get a thorough distribution of the salt.

Molding and Pressing the Cheese

Once the cheese has been drained, milled, and salted, you will move the curds to a cheese mold or press for further draining and molding. Not all cheese will require this, but most hard cheeses do. As the word indicates, a cheese mold will determine the shape of your cheese. *Cheese molds and presses are described in Chapter 1.*

There are many kinds of cheese that do not need to be pressed; soft cheese, semisoft cheese, and mold- and bacteria-ripened cheese, for the most part, do not need to be pressed. Cheese that does not need to be pressed will be placed in a mold lined with cheesecloth. You will lightly pack the curds into the mold. Be careful not to handle the curds too roughly or pack them too tightly, as you are still trying to retain butterfat, and excess handling and weight will force some of the butterfat out of the curds.

You will press cheese to squeeze the curd with weight, similar to how you would squeeze water from a sponge. Pressure is put on the curd to force out any excess moisture. Some cheese is pressed with light weight for hours, while some harder cheeses are pressed for days by increasing amounts of weight. The amount of weight you use will determine the final texture of your cheese.

The operation to press cheese is pretty straightforward:

1. Line a cheese mold with cheesecloth.

2. Put the mold into a pan that will catch the draining whey.

3. Spoon the curds into the mold.

4. Cover the top of the curds with a piece of cheesecloth.

5. Lay the follower (the piece that snugly fits into the opening in the top of mold) on top of the cheesecloth.

6. At this point, make sure that your covering cheesecloth is tight and not bunched up anywhere on top.

7. Apply weight as per cheese recipe.

Most of the recipes will call for gradually increasing weight over a period of time. If you press too hard from the very start of the process, you will force out too much of the important butterfat, and your cheese will not drain properly.

You will also probably be required to flip the cheese. To flip it, you will remove the cheese from the mold and unwrap the cheesecloth. Flip the cheese over and put it back in the cheesecloth. Put the cheesecloth-covered cheese back in the mold and continue pressing.

Drying the Cheese

Some cheese will require some extra time to dry after being pressed. Again, this step varies in time depending on the kind of cheese you are making. For the drying process, you will place your drained and molded cheese on a drying mat and allow it to sit, usually at room temperature, for a specific period of time.

Further Preparation

After the cheese has been allowed to dry for several days, there are several ways you can prepare your cheese for further aging. The preparation process is a step taken to protect the outside of the cheese as it ages. There are three basic ways to accomplish this preparation:

Bandaging

Bandaging is exactly what it sounds like: Cloth bandages made from butter muslin are wrapped around the cheese. Bandaging is employed to help form a rind on the outside of the cheese.

To bandage a molded cheese:

1. Cut two double layers of butter muslin that are slightly larger than the top and bottom form of the cheese.

2. Cut a piece of butter muslin that will wrap completely around the side of the cheese.

3. Rub the outside of the cheese with a very thin layer of a solid organic vegetable shortening or lard. This will help the muslin cling to the cheese.

4. Follow recipe directions on storing cheese from this point on. Each cheese will have its own specific requirements.

Natural rind

Even if you do not bandage the cheese, a natural rind will form. The rind is the dry outer layer that forms on the cheese as it ages. The moisture evaporates from the outer layer and it hardens, forming a protective crust on the outside of the cheese.

If you allow the cheese to form this natural rind, you have to make sure no undesirable mold forms on the outside of the cheese. To protect against this, it is best to clean the surface of the cheese every so often. To clean the cheese, you can wipe it with a damp piece of cheesecloth that has been dipped in vinegar or a brine solution.

Cheese wax

Cheese wax was defined in Chapter 1. Cheese wax is the preferred method of protecting cheese that you want to be softer and have a little more moisture. Some cheeses form a very good natural rind if they are made in larger quantities, but these cheeses should be waxed if you make them in smaller blocks. Swiss cheese is a good example of this. If you make cheese in blocks that are fewer than 2 pounds, you will want to consider waxing them to protect against excessive drying during the aging process.

To wax cheese, you will need:

Double boiler with the inner pot being the pot that will hold the wax (This pot will become a dedicated wax pot, as it will be nearly impossible to clean it for cooking purposes after you have made wax)

Thermometer

Natural-bristle brush

Latex or rubber gloves

Cheese wax

Process

1. Cool the cheese in the refrigerator. As you are performing this function of waxing the cheese as a part of the cheese-making process, most cheese will be at room temperature prior to this step.

2. Melt wax in double boiler.

3. Use thermometer to check temperature of wax; it should get to 250°. This temperature will kill any surface bacteria on the cheese.

4. Clean the cheese by wiping it with a damp piece of cheesecloth that has been dipped in vinegar or a brine solution.

5. At this point, you can either dip your cheese in the wax or brush the wax onto the cheese.

To dip the cheese:

1. Wearing gloves, hold the cheese by one side.

2. With a quick in-and-out motion, dip the cheese into the wax.

3. Allow the wax to harden. It should harden almost immediately.

4. Repeat process for the other side of the cheese.

5. Repeat process, giving the cheese two coats of wax.

To brush wax on cheese:

1. Brush wax lightly on one surface of the cheese.

2. Allow wax to harden.

3. Turn cheese over and brush wax on exposed surface.

4. Repeat process, allowing wax to harden one surface at a time until you have given the cheese two coats of wax.

It is a good idea to label the cheese that you wax so you know what type of cheese is beneath the wax. You can do this by simply brushing a thin coat of wax over a prepared paper label onto the waxed cheese.

When you are ready to eat the cheese, the wax is simply peeled off. You can then re-use the wax by melting it down and straining it through a piece of cheesecloth or butter muslin.

Aging the Cheese

Aging cheese can take anywhere from 24 hours to five or six years. The cheeses you will make initially will be the kinds that age for a short period of time. This is a good way to start because it is nearly instant gratification when you taste your wonderful Mozzarella or delicious cream cheese. A longer wait will be in store for you as you wait a week to eat your fantastic feta. Beyond that, other cheeses you make, such as Monterey Jack, might age for one to four months. A sharp provolone or cheddar could even keep you waiting for a year.

To properly age cheese, you need to be able to keep it in a controlled environment with a sharp eye on temperature and humidity. These controls are necessary to allow the mold and bacteria that give the cheese flavor the best chance to grow.

Most recipes you use will call for you to age your cheese in a location that is between 45° and 60°, with a humidity level between 75 and 95 percent. If you are not equipped with such a "cave" that is suitable to maintain these conditions, it is suggested that you keep the cheese in a place that does not go above 68°. A household refrigerator is not recommended, though a dedicated refrigerator used solely for cheese is acceptable.

There are several other processes you will learn in the coming chapters that have to do with specific cheeses. Some cheese requires that you employ a smoking procedure while other cheeses need acidity testing. These processes will be covered when making the cheese that they are specific to are described.

What is described above is the basic process for making cheese. Armed with this information and several key ingredients such as milk and a starter, you can make countless kinds of cheese. This book is arranged to go from the simplest recipes to the most difficult, and this section on cheese is no different. The best place to begin to learn to make cheese is by making soft cheese. Get ready to toast some bagels.

CASE STUDY: SUSAN BROWN

Amaltheia Organic Dairy, LLC
www.amaltheiadairy.com

Amaltheia Organic Dairy has been a commercial dairy for eight years and makes organic, award-winning goat's milk cheese, including chèvre, ricotta, and feta. Susan Brown became involved in cheese making because she loved goat's milk products. She said goat's milk is good for digestion, weight management, bones, and general health.

"What we enjoy most about making cheese is that we love to make high-quality cheese," Brown said. "People love our cheese. The hardest thing about making cheese is adjusting for [variables] such as fat content and changes that come with the time of the year. My favorite cheese to make is goat feta. Our handmade goat feta has been featured on the Food Network. My favorite cheese to eat is Amaltheia Organic Dairy Spiced Pepper.

"A word of advice to those who are just getting started in making cheese? Keep trying to get it right," Brown said.

CHAPTER 11

Making Soft Cheeses

You have already made several types of soft cheeses based on recipes in chapters 5 and 8. Making soft cheese is a wonderful way to begin to learn the cheese-making process, as most soft cheese is relatively easy to make, and you can learn a few of the basic techniques as you receive that near-instant gratification.

Most soft cheeses require little or no pressing, aging, or specific temperature and humidity control that hard cheeses do. Soft cheeses require little in the way of special equipment.

You will find that once you learn the basic techniques of making soft cheese, you will be able to experiment by adding herbs, spices, and other flavors that will make each of the basic recipes your own.

Before you break out the bagels for your first batch of homemade cream cheese, it is important to cover a few tips that relate to all of the recipes that will follow:

- All recipes in this section call for the milk to be heated in an indirect manner, such as in a hot water bath or in a double boiler.

- Unless otherwise specified, always drain your cheese at room temperature.

- Depending on the kind of milk you use (skim, low-fat, or whole), you will get about 1 ½ to 2 pounds of cheese from 1 gallon of milk. The more butterfat, the greater yield of cheese.

- Soft cheese will keep for up to two weeks in the refrigerator if it is stored in a well-sealed container.

Cream Cheese

Cream cheese is a favorite. It is third best-selling natural cheese in the United States after Mozzarella and cheddar. It is easy to make and pleases many palates. Here are a couple of recipes for cream cheese. One can be made with no cooking, and the other is made with very little cooking. Both recipes require about 12 to 24 hours to make.

Easy cream cheese

Ingredients

1 quart milk (Whole milk is best for this recipe)
1 quart heavy cream
½ tsp powdered mesophilic starter (If you are using a prepared starter, use 4 ounces)
¼ tablet vegetable rennet dissolved in ¼ cup of cool, unchlorinated water (If you are using liquid rennet, use two drops)
Salt (optional)

Directions

1. Whisk the milk and cream together in a stainless-steel mixing bowl or pot.

2. Place the pot in a warm water bath and allow the mixture to warm to 72°.

3. Scatter the mesophilic starter over the top of the milk/cream and stir it until it is thoroughly combined.

4. Add the rennet/water mixture to the milk/cream and stir well to ensure it is well-mixed.

5. Cover the mixture and allow it to ripen at room temperature for 24 hours. Make sure the mixture is out of drafts and the sun.

6. After 24 hours, the mixture will have the consistency of yogurt.

7. Line a colander with a large, doubled piece of cheesecloth. Make sure the cloth is large enough that you will be able to bring the corners together in a bag for the cheese to drain.

8. Transfer the cheese to the cheesecloth-lined colander.

9. Bring the corners of the cheesecloth together and tie them so you can hang the bag to drain at room temperature. Make sure you save the whey.

10. Allow the bag to drain for about 12 hours, or until the whey stops running off the curd.

11. At this point you should have a fairly solid mass of curd. That curd is your cream cheese.

12. Place the cheese into a bowl and stir in salt, if you are so inclined. You can also mix in any other flavor that might tickle your taste buds.

Cream cheese II

This recipe calls for the curd to be cooked to a slightly higher temperature, and the cheese that results from this recipe is a little drier than the cheese you will get from the easy cream cheese recipe listed above. This cheese is also better to use in cheesecake recipes.

Ingredients
2 quarts light cream
½ tsp powdered mesophilic starter (If you are using a prepared starter, use 4 ounces)

¼ tablet vegetable rennet dissolved in ¼ cup of cool, unchlorinated water (If you are using liquid rennet, use two drops)

Salt (optional)

Directions

1. In a double boiler or a hot water bath, bring the temperature of the cream to 86°.

2. Scatter the mesophilic starter over the top of the cream and stir it until it is thoroughly combined.

3. Add the rennet/water mixture to the cream and stir well to ensure it is well-mixed.

4. Cover the mixture and allow it to ripen at room temperature for 12 hours. Make sure that the mixture is out of drafts and the sun.

5. In a double boiler, heat the curd to 125°.

6. Line a colander with a large, doubled piece of cheesecloth. Make sure the cloth is large enough that you will be able to bring the corners together in a bag for the cheese to drain.

7. Transfer the cheese to the cheesecloth-lined colander.

8. Bring the corners of the cheesecloth together and tie them so you can hang the bag to drain. Make sure you save the whey.

9. Allow the bag to drain at room temperature for about 12 hours, or until the whey stops running off the curd.

10. At this point you should have a fairly solid mass of curd. That curd is your cream cheese.

11. Place the cheese into a bowl and stir in salt, if you are so inclined. You can also mix in any other herbs or seasonings you wish.

Neufchatel

The name "Neufchatel" refers to the town of Neufchatel-en-Bray in Normandy, France. Neufchatel-en-Bray is a rainy (humid) and temperate place, and this is a cheese that (in its native form) is truly a product of its environment. The climate of Neufchatel-en-Bray allows for lush grasses on which the local cows graze, and this diet gives their milk a particular character. The climate also sets the atmosphere for the aging of the cheese. Notice in most cheese recipes that require aging that specific temperatures and humidity levels are suggested. In most cases, these suggested temperatures and humidity levels are the result of the environments where the cheese was initially developed.

You may buy Neufchatel in your local grocery store when you want a low-fat cream cheese. Neufchatel is lower in fat content than cream cheese because it is made with whole milk as opposed to cream. Neufchatel is different from cream cheese in a couple of other ways, as well. Neufchatel is pressed to expel moisture, making it somewhat drier than cream cheese. Neufchatel is allowed to ripen for a little longer than cream cheese, and that tends to make it slightly more flavorful. How flavorful it is depends on how long it has been allowed to ripen. It will range from very mild to sharp and salty. True Neufchatel is ripened with a small amount of white surface mold.

Here are two recipes for Neufchatel. The first recipe is going to make a cheese very similar to the Neufchatel that you might buy in your local grocery store, and it tastes like that light cream cheese you are familiar with. The second recipe will produce a more traditional Neufchatel, as it will be aged with *Penicillium candidum*. The second Neufchatel recipe here is a more advanced cheese-making recipe, but it is placed here to present a challenge, as well as to give you an idea as to the flexibility of many of these cheese-making recipes.

Neufchatel I

Ingredients

1 gallon whole milk

1 pint heavy cream

½ tsp powdered mesophilic starter (If you are using a prepared starter, use 4 ounces)

¼ tablet vegetable rennet dissolved in ¼ cup of cool, unchlorinated water (If you are using liquid rennet, use two drops)

Directions

1. Whisk together whole milk and cream in a stainless-steel mixing bowl or pot.
2. Place bowl with milk/cream mixture in a warm water bath to bring the temperature to 72°.
3. Stir mesophilic starter into the milk/cream, making sure to mix well.
4. Stir 1 tsp of the diluted rennet into the milk/cream.

Precise measurements

Note the measurement of only 1 tsp of the prepared rennet measurement. In this recipe, if you do not add enough rennet, your curd will be runny and may flow right through the cheese-cloth when you drain it. If you add too much rennet, you will end up with a rubbery mass of curd. You may find that you will need to experiment a little and adjust to the milk that you use. Because not all milk is alike, it is important that you keep notes and keep track of precise amounts of ingredients you use to adjust for the milk and cream you use.

5. Cover the milk/cream and let ripen at room temperature for 12 to 20 hours. The mixture will develop a yogurt-like consistency.

6. Line a colander with a large, doubled piece of cheesecloth. Make sure the cloth is large enough that you will be able to bring the corners together in a bag for the cheese to drain. Place the colander over a pot to catch the whey.

7. Ladle the curds into the cheesecloth-lined colander.

8. Allow the curds to drain for about 20 minutes.

9. Fold the cheesecloth over the top of the curds and place a plate on top of the curds.

10. Place a weight (5 pounds will do) on top of the plate to press the curd.

11. Cover the draining curd and refrigerate for 12 hours.

12. Remove the curds from the cheesecloth and place into a small bowl.

13. Mix by hand until smooth, adding salt, herbs, or seasonings to taste.

14. The Neufchatel will keep in a sealed container in the refrigerator for up to two weeks. The cheese will firm up a little when it is refrigerated.

Neufchatel II

This recipe is closer to the truly French Neufchatel. The cheese must ripen for seven to ten days and will take you close to two weeks to make. Regardless, this cheese is still relatively easy to make, and the resulting product is wonderfully tasty.

Ingredients

1 gallon whole milk

1 pint heavy cream

½ tsp powdered mesophilic starter (If you are using a prepared starter, use 4 ounces)

¼ tablet vegetable rennet dissolved in ¼ cup of cool, unchlorinated water (If you are using liquid rennet, use two drops)

¹/₈ tsp *Penicillium candidum*

Directions

1. Whisk together whole milk and cream in a stainless-steel mixing bowl or pot.

2. Place bowl with milk/cream mixture in a warm water bath to bring the temperature to 80°.

3. Stir mesophilic starter into the milk/cream, making sure to mix well.

4. Stir in *Penicillium candidum*, making sure to mix well.

5. Gently stir 1 tsp of the diluted rennet into the milk/cream.

6. Cover the milk/cream and let ripen at room temperature for 12 to 20 hours. The mixture will develop a yogurt-like consistency.

7. Line a colander with a large, doubled piece of cheesecloth. Make sure the cloth is large enough that you will be able to bring the corners together in a bag for the cheese to drain. Place the colander over a pot to catch the whey.

8. Ladle the curds into the cheesecloth-lined colander.

9. Allow the curds to drain for about 20 minutes.

10. Bring the corners of the cheesecloth together and tie into a bag.

11. Hang the bag of curds over the pot and allow it to drain at room temperature for 12 hours. The whey should have stopped draining from the bag at this point.

12. Place the cheesecloth bag of curds back into the colander and put the colander over a bowl.

13. Place a plate on top of the curds and put a 5-pound weight on the plate to further press the curds.

14. Refrigerate and allow the curd to drain for another 12 hours.

15. Remove the curds from the cheesecloth and place them in molds in the shape you would like your cheese to be.

16. When the cheese is firm, remove it from the mold and place it in a "cave" at 45° and 90 percent humidity for seven to ten days. At this point, your cheese should have a fine coat of white mold on it.

17. Remove the cheese from the cave and wrap it in wax paper.

18. Allow the cheese to ripen in the "cave" for another three weeks.

19. The cheese will keep in your refrigerator for up to four weeks.

Cheese Molds

Some cheeses have shapes that they are traditionally molded into, and the reasoning behind the shapes and molds varies with the cheese. Neufchatel is traditionally molded into a heart-shaped mold because it is said that the coquettish daughters of French cheese makers would make the Neufchatel into the shape of a heart as a gift for British soldiers during the Hundred Years' War. This is a very fanciful example of why a cheese has its traditional shape.

A more practical example of why a cheese is the shape it is can be explained by cheddar cheese. Cheddar cheese is, more often than not, made as a "wheel" because it requires a great deal of pressure to be put on it over an extended period of time when it is being made. Cylinders are able to withstand a lot of pressure and retain their shape better than any other shape.

Mozzarella is commonly made in the shape of a ball because it requires no pressing and is kneaded by hand. As Mozzarella reaches its desired consistency, it is merely made into a ball and put into cold-water brine for finishing. In this sense, your hands become the final mold.

Chèvre

"Chèvre" is the French word for "goat" and chèvre is — you guessed it — goat cheese. Chévre is a cheese that is extremely popular among artisan cheese makers because it is relatively easy to make and wonderful to eat. Like cream cheese and

Neufchatel, once you get the hang of making chèvre, you can flavor it with herbs and spices and give it your own spin.

Working with goat's milk is a little different from working with the milk of a cow. You may recall from Chapter 2 that goat's milk has a lower fat content than cow's milk, which makes chèvre a slightly different cheese from cream cheese, though the procedure in making them is quite similar.

There are several different ways to make chèvre described here. Two of them are very easy, and one of the recipes will employ a starter that is used specifically when working with goat's milk. Like the Neufchatel recipes, one recipe will describe how to make mold-ripened chèvre.

Working with Goat's Milk

Goat's milk produces a much softer curd than cow's milk, so you need to be very gentle in working with it. When stirring, cutting, or transferring the curd, do so with a little more care than you might normally use when working with other milks.

Chèvre I

One of the ingredients discussed in Chapter 2 was acid, which is used in a number of different cheese recipes to aid in the coagulation of milk. In this recipe, an acid is the only ingredient used to coagulate the milk. One might wonder if this was the original way that chèvre was first made.

Ingredients
1 gallon whole goat's milk
Up to ½ cup cider vinegar (You can also use lemon juice)

Directions
1. Pour milk into a stainless-steel, double-boiler pot.

2. Gradually heat the milk to 185°.

3. Stir the milk frequently.

4. Hold the temperature at 185° for ten minutes.

5. Remove the pot from the heat and allow the milk to cool to 100° by putting the pot in a cool water bath. You can let it sit at room temperature, but the cool water will allow the milk to cool much quicker.

6. Slowly stir in ¼ cup of the vinegar.

7. The milk should begin to coagulate. The curd will appear as little balls of cottage cheese as it separates from the whey. If this does not occur, slowly stir in another ¼ cup of vinegar.

8. Line a colander with a large, doubled piece of cheesecloth. Make sure the cloth is large enough that you will be able to bring the corners together in a bag for the cheese to drain. Place the colander over a pot to catch the whey.

9. Once the curds have separated from the whey, use a ladle to transfer the curds to the cheesecloth-lined colander.

10. If you have a hard time getting all of the curds with the ladle, you can gently pour the curds and whey into the colander.

11. Allow the curds to drain in the colander for ten minutes.

12. Bring the corners of the cheesecloth together and tie into a bag.

13. Hang the bag of curds over the pot and allow it to drain at room temperature for six hours or until it reaches the desired consistency.

14. Transfer the cheese to a bowl. You may now add herbs or other seasonings. A suggestion might be a little salt and then, after you have formed your chèvre, roll it in some cracked black peppercorns. What you decide to flavor your cheese with is a matter of personal preference.

15. Chèvre is best served fresh. It will keep in a sealed container in your refrigerator for up to a week but should be consumed as soon as possible.

Chèvre II

This version of chèvre is a little more complicated than the chèvre recipe above, but is more along the lines of the cream cheese recipes offered earlier in this chapter, as it employs a starter and rennet.

Ingredients

1 gallon whole goat's milk

¼ tsp powdered mesophilic starter (If you are using a prepared starter, use 4 ounces)

$^1/_8$ tsp calcium chloride dissolved in ¼ cup cool, unchlorinated water

¼ tablet vegetable rennet dissolved in ¼ cup of cool, unchlorinated water (If you are using liquid rennet, use two drops)

Directions

1. Pour the milk into a stainless-steel bowl or pot.

2. Place the bowl of milk into a warm water bath to bring the temperature of the milk to 85°.

3. Add the mesophilic starter and stir well.

4. Add calcium chloride mixture and stir well.

5. Add 2 tbsp of the rennet mixture. Remember, if you are using powdered or rennet tablets, allow 20 to 30 minutes for the rennet to fully dissolve.

6. Stir gently.

7. Cover mixture and allow it to sit at room temperature for 18 to 24 hours.

8. At this point, the curds will be a thick, yogurt-like consistency.

9. Line a colander with a large, doubled piece of cheesecloth. Make sure the cloth is large enough that you will be able to bring the corners together in a bag for the cheese to drain. Place the colander over a pot to catch the whey.

10. Use a ladle to transfer the curds to the cheesecloth-lined colander.

11. If you have a hard time getting all of the curds with the ladle, you can gently pour the curds and whey into the colander.

12. Allow the curds to drain in the colander for ten minutes.

13. Bring the corners of the cheesecloth together and tie into a bag.

14. Hang the bag of curds over the pot and allow it to drain at room temperature for six hours or until it reaches the desired consistency.

15. Transfer the cheese to a bowl. You may now add herbs or other seasonings.

16. This chèvre will keep in an airtight container in your refrigerator for up to two weeks.

Chèvre III

As you did with Neufchatel, you can make a mold-ripened chèvre. This recipe is so good that it will turn you into a chèvre snob, and you may never be able to go back to plain, unmolded cheese again. This mold-ripened chèvre has the wonder-filled name Sainte Maure de Touraine and was developed in the Loire Valley in France. To make this cheese in the traditional way, you would form it in the shape of a log with a piece of straw running through the length of the middle of the cheese. The straw allows air to penetrate the center of the log as the cheese ripens. When this cheese is fully ripe, it has the appearance of a rolled-up piece of wool, but do not let the appearance fool you. The texture of the cheese is delightfully soft and creamy.

Ingredients

1 gallon whole goat's milk

¼ tsp powdered mesophilic starter (If you are using a prepared starter, use 4 ounces)

$^1/_8$ tsp calcium chloride dissolved in ¼ cup cool, unchlorinated water

¼ tablet vegetable rennet dissolved in ¼ cup of cool, unchlorinated water (If you are using liquid rennet, use two drops)

$^1/_8$ tsp *Penicillium candidum*

Directions

1. Pour goat's milk into a stainless-steel mixing bowl or pot.

2. Place bowl with milk in a warm water bath to bring the temperature to 85°.

3. Stir mesophilic starter into the milk, making sure to mix well.

4. Add calcium chloride mixture and stir well.

5. Stir in *Penicillium candidum* and stir well.

6. Gently stir 2 tbsp of the diluted rennet into the milk.

7. Cover mixture and allow it to sit at room temperature for 18 to 24 hours.

8. At this point, the curds will be a thick, yogurt-like consistency.

9. Line a colander with a large, doubled piece of cheesecloth. Make sure the cloth is large enough that you will be able to bring the corners together in a bag for the cheese to drain. Place the colander over a pot to catch the whey.

10. Use a ladle to transfer the curds to the cheesecloth-lined colander.

11. If you have a hard time getting all of the curds with the ladle, you can gently pour the curds and whey into the colander.

12. Allow the curds to drain in the colander for ten minutes.

13. Spoon the curds into individual cheese molds. The traditional mold for Sainte Maure is a cheese log that is about 2 inches in diameter and about 6 inches long. You can, however, use any type of small mold you choose.

14. Place the logs on a draining mat. Allow the molds to drain at room temperature for two days.

15. Remove the cheese from the molds and place on cheese mat. The cheese may have already begun to develop some fuzzy mold.

16. To protect your cheese from any unwanted airborne bacteria, you can place the mats with the logs in a gallon-sized plastic bag. Inflate the bag and seal it. The bag can now sit at room temperature out of the sun to age for two to three days. You will start to notice mold fuzz growing on your cheese, which is good.

17. After two or three days, you can move your aging cheese in the bag to your refrigerator and let it age there for two or three more weeks.

18. You can eat the mold-ripened chèvre any time after the mold starts to grow, but for the full effect of this delicious cheese, try to hold off until the cheese has had a chance to grow a good coat of mold for a couple of weeks in your refrigerator. The mold will appear as a fine coat of white "fur."

19. Make sure that the crackers or bread that you enjoy this cheese on are of excellent quality. Also, do not forget the wine.

Alternative Method of Inoculating Cheese with *Penicillium candidum*

You will learn more about mold-ripened cheese in Chapter 15 of this book. For now, you can choose to introduce the *Penicillium candidum* in the manner described above, or you can apply mold to the surface after you take it out of the cheese molds. To do this, you omit the step of adding the *Penicillium candidum* early in the process.

- Ten to 15 hours prior to applying the *Penicillium candidum* to the surface of the cheese, you should have dissolved ⅛ tsp of the mold powder in 1 quart of cool, sterilized, unchlorinated water.

- After you remove the cheese from the log-shaped mold, lightly salt the all surfaces of the cheese.

- The mold powder may have come pre-packaged. If so, follow the package directions for re-hydrating the powder.

- Using an atomizer, lightly spray the surface of the cheese with the *Penicillium candidum* preparation.

- Allow the cheese to ripen for 14 days at 52° with a relative humidity of 95 percent. At this point, a thick coat of white mold should have developed on the surface of the cheese.

- Wrap cheese in wax paper. It may be refrigerated for up to two weeks.

Fromage Blanc

Fromage blanc is French for "white cheese." Consequently, if you seek a recipe to make fromage blanc, you could come across a great number of variations for this French "white cheese." The French word for cheese, "fromage," is actually of Greek origin. The Greek word "formos" does not mean cheese, but is the word used to describe the straw baskets used to drain cheese.

Fromage blanc is a soft and spreadable cheese similar to cream cheese, Neufchatel, and chèvre. Like those cheeses, there are a number of ways you can go about making them.

Fromage blanc I

Ingredients
½ gallon whole milk
1 cup heavy cream
1 pint homemade cultured buttermilk
2 tbsp cider vinegar (lemon juice is also acceptable)
Salt (optional)

Directions
1. In a stainless-steel double boiler, mix milk and cream.

2. In a stainless-steel mixing bowl, whisk together buttermilk and vinegar.

3. Stir buttermilk/vinegar mixture into milk/cream mixture.

4. Slowly heat to 180°.

5. Stir mixture occasionally.

6. When mixture reaches 180°, remove from heat.

7. Allow mixture to sit undisturbed for ten minutes. Curds should have formed at this point.

8. Line a colander with a large, doubled piece of cheesecloth. Make sure the cloth is large enough that you will be able to bring the corners together in a bag for the cheese to drain. Place the colander over a pot to catch the whey.

9. Use a ladle to gently transfer the formed curds into the cheesecloth-lined colander.

10. Allow curds to drain in colander for about ten minutes.

11. Bring and tie corners of cheesecloth together to form a bag.

12. Hang bag over pot for further draining.

13. Allow to drain at room temperature for about six hours or until desired consistency is reached.

14. Salt to taste if desired.

15. Cheese can be refrigerated in a sealed container for up to a week.

Fromage blanc II

Cheese supply companies sell a fromage blanc starter, which is a mesophilic starter that usually comes as a mixture of starter bacteria and rennet. Fromage blanc is a very mild cheese that tastes very similar to ricotta. The Fromage blanc starter allows for the formation of a curd without a fully ripened taste. You will need to use this starter in the recipe that follows.

Ingredients

1 gallon whole milk

½ tsp fromage blanc starter (or a pre-packaged starter from which you will follow package directions for adding to milk)

Salt (optional)

Directions

1. Pour the milk into a hot water bath and allow it to warm to 85°.

2. Add fromage blanc starter and mix well.

3. Cover the mixture and allow it to ripen at room temperature for 12 hours.

4. Line a colander with a large, doubled piece of cheesecloth. Make sure the cloth is large enough that you will be able to bring the corners together in a bag for the cheese to drain. Place the colander over a pot to catch the whey.

5. Gently ladle the curds into the cheesecloth-lined colander.

6. Allow curds to drain in colander for about ten minutes.

7. Bring and tie corners of cheesecloth together to form a bag.

8. Hang bag over pot for further draining.

9. Allow to drain for about six hours or until desired consistency is reached.

10. Salt to taste if desired.

11. Cheese can be refrigerated in a sealed container for up to a week.

All of the soft cheeses described in this chapter thus far have been relatively similar in nature. Though some have been mold-ripened and others have been produced using only an acid as opposed to a starter, they all have been simple to make.

Other soft cheese recipes that you might find worth trying if you are interested in pursuing more variations on the cream cheese-type spread are queso blanco, paneer, and Bondon cheese. All of these cheeses are quick soft cheeses that are made in very much the same way as cream cheese, chèvre, and Neufchatel. Just like the other cream cheese varieties mentioned, a starter is added to milk, rennet is added, and the milk is allowed to sit and form curd. The curd is drained, and you have cheese. This method of making cheese harkens back to the earliest days of cheese when that proverbial camel walked across the desert with a saddlebag full of ripening milk.

It is now time to move on in the cheese-making process, as the curd is cut and a few more steps are added along the way. The next few recipes will continue with what will still be called soft cheese, but you will notice that some new techniques are going to be added to the process.

Leipäjuusto

Here is a cheese that is as much fun to make as it is to eat, especially if you enjoy using your outdoor grill. Leipäjuusto is the original grilled cheese and translates to "bread cheese." It is called this because when you are done making it, it resembles a round of unleavened bread. You can tell the kids that this bread is also known as Finnish squeaky bread. You will understand this as you eat it because it really does squeak.

The recipe given here calls for cow's milk. However, it would not be unusual to find this cheese made with reindeer's milk in Finland. If you happen to have access to a reindeer or moose, go ahead and use that milk.

Ingredients
1 ½ gallons whole milk
¼ tablet vegetable rennet dissolved in ¼ cup of cool, unchlorinated water (If you are using liquid rennet, use two drops)
Salt (to taste)
Seasoning (to taste)

Directions
1. Pour milk into a stainless-steel pot of a double boiler.

2. Slowly heat milk to 100°.

3. Gently stir in the dissolved rennet mixture, making sure to thoroughly mix into milk.

4. Remove pot of milk from the heat.

5. Cover pot of milk and allow milk to ripen for 30 minutes.

6. Line a colander with a large, doubled piece of cheesecloth. Make sure the cloth is large enough that you will be able to bring the corners together in a bag for the cheese to drain. Place the colander over a pot to catch the whey.

7. Gently pour the curds into the cheesecloth-lined colander.

8. Allow curds to drain in colander for about ten minutes.

9. Bring and tie corners of cheesecloth together to form a bag.

10. Twist the bag around to gently squeeze whey from the curds.

11. Untie the bag and transfer the cheese to a bowl.

12. Season to taste. Note that Leipäjuusto, like many soft cheeses, has a fairly plain taste. Leipäjuusto will easily take on any flavor or seasoning that you add to it. When you season the cheese, consider what you might be serving it with and complement it. Some prefer just adding a little salt, but other options include garlic, lemon zest, caraway, freshly ground black pepper, or hot dry mustard powder.

13. Use your hands to form the cheese into a flat pancake. It will be about 9 inches in diameter.

14. You can now choose to broil or grill the cheese.

To broil:

1. Place the round of cheese on a broiler pan that allows for drainage. There should be a pan underneath the slotted pan to catch additional whey that drains during broiling.

2. Broil for three minutes or until the cheese develops a nice brown top crust. Keep an eye on it.

3. Remove from broiler and place the cheese on a plate.

4. Leipäjuusto is traditionally cut into bite-sized cubes.

To grill:

1. Place round of cheese on a water-soaked, wooden grilling board. If you have slotted grilling board, all the better. In lieu of a grilling board, you can use the same kind of broiling pan noted above.

2. Place board/pan on grill and cover.

3. Grill until cheese develops a golden brown crust. Time will depend on how hot your fire is.

4. Remove from heat and transfer to plate to be cut into bite-sized cubes.

Whether you broil the cheese or grill it, Leipäjuusto is great with a hearty rye bread.

Cottage Cheese

If you have never experienced homemade cottage cheese, you are in for what could be the biggest treat this book has to offer. A fun fact: Cottage cheese is so named because it is a cheese that is easily made at home, or in your own cottage. It is about as basic as you can get when it comes to making cheese. You will find, however, that the cottage cheese you make at home is quite different from the cottage cheese that you buy in your local grocery store. Fresh homemade cottage cheese is so vastly superior to store-bought, commercially produced cottage cheese that you may well abandon the store-bought product forever after you master this simple process.

One reason you will be convinced of the superior nature of homemade cottage cheese is related to an issue that was discussed in Chapter 6. If you examine the ingredients of most of the cottage cheese that sits in the dairy case of your local grocery store, you may come across a list of ingredients that looks something like this:

Cultured fat-free milk, buttermilk, nonfat dry milk, cream, salt, citric acid, lactic acid, phosphoric acid, natural flavoring, guar gum, mono and diglycerides, xanthan gum, carob bean gum, titanium dioxide (artificial color), maltodextrin, cultured dextrose, potassium sorbate, calcium chloride, enzymes.

You might well ask yourself why a product made with milk and cream that is white requires an artificial color. The recipes in this book do not require phosphoric acid, natural flavoring, guar gum, mono and diglycerides, xanthan gum, carob bean gum, titanium dioxide (artificial color), maltodextrin, cultured dextrose, or potassium sorbate.

What follows here are several recipes for both large-curd and small-curd cottage cheese, and there are several options for making both kinds of this cheese. As you become more experienced in your cheese making and understand some of the basic techniques, you can experiment with developing your own techniques for making this popular cheese that people have been making in their own kitchens (and saddlebags) for hundreds of years.

After the cottage-cheese recipes, you will find recipes for items that are very similar in nature and origin to cottage cheese: pot cheese and farmer's cheese. Like cottage cheese, these are items that have been made by home cheese makers for hundreds of years.

Small-curd cottage cheese

Ingredients
1 gallon milk (whole, low-fat, or skim)

$^1/_8$ tsp calcium chloride dissolved in ¼ cup of cool, unchlorinated water (If you are using farm-fresh milk, you may omit this ingredient)

½ tsp powdered mesophilic starter (If you are using a prepared starter, use 4 ounces)

2 to 4 tbsp of heavy cream (optional)

Salt (optional)

Directions
1. Pour the milk in a stainless-steel pot.

2. Place the pot in a warm water bath and bring the temperature of the milk to 72°.

3. Stir the calcium chloride into the milk, making sure to mix it thoroughly.

4. Gently stir the mesophilic starter into the milk, making sure to mix it thoroughly.

5. Cover the pot and let the mixture sit at room temperature for about 16 hours.

6. At this point, you should have a firm curd that is about the consistency of custard. A knife inserted into the curd should produce a clean break. Likewise, you can test the consistency of the curd by inserting your finger. *See instructions on cutting the curds in Chapter 10.*

7. Cut curds into ¼- to ½-inch cubes.

8. Allow the curds to settle for 20 minutes, allowing for some of the whey to separate from the curds and rise to the top.

9. In a double boiler, very slowly heat the curds and whey to 110°. The temperature should increase from about 72° to 110° over a 45-minute period.

10. During the heating process, the curds should be stirred very gently every five minutes. Your goal with the stirring is to bring the curds that are on the bottom to the top as you evenly heat them.

11. Hold the temperature between 110° and 112° for 30 minutes.

12. As you heat the curds, you will notice that they are expelling more whey and becoming more firm.

13. After 30 minutes, you can test the firmness of the curd by squeezing one in your fingers. If the curd feels mushy (like custard), you should continue to cook it a little more. If the curd feels somewhat firm, you are ready to move on.

14. Once you have a somewhat firm curd, remove the pot from the heat.

15. Allow the curds and whey to sit for about 15 minutes. The curds will settle to the bottom of the pot as the whey will rise to the top.

16. Line a colander with a large, doubled piece of cheesecloth. Make sure the cloth is large enough that you will be able to bring the corners together in a bag for the cheese to drain. Place the colander over a pot to catch the whey.

17. Gently pour the curds into the cheesecloth-lined colander.

18. Allow curds to drain in colander for about ten minutes.

19. Bring and tie corners of cheesecloth together to form a bag.

20. Prepare a large pot of cold water.

21. After the bag of curds has drained for 15 minutes, dip the bag into the cold water.

22. Place the bag of curds back into the colander and allow it to drain for ten minutes.

23. Untie the bag and transfer the curds to a bowl.

24. By this point, the curds should be very firm.

25. Break the curds up by hand into smaller pieces. *See instructions for milling curds in Chapter 10.*

26. If you plan on adding salt or other herbs or spices to your cottage cheese, this is the time to do it.

27. Some may enjoy the cottage cheese as it is at this point, though you will notice that it is somewhat drier than the cottage cheese you buy in the supermarket. If you enjoy a creamier cottage cheese, you can add a little heavy cream just before you serve it. Note that you should not add the cream unless you plan on serving the cottage cheese right away, as the curd will soak up the cream and will alter the texture of your cottage cheese.

Large-curd cottage cheese

You will notice a few small differences between this recipe and the recipe for small-curd cottage cheese above, but the primary difference here is the use of rennet. The rennet in this recipe aids in the coagulation of the milk and gives it a moderately larger curd. The use of rennet also means that you will not have to let the milk ripen for nearly as long as the small-curd variety of this cheese.

Ingredients

1 gallon milk (whole, low-fat, or skim)

$^1/_8$ tsp calcium chloride dissolved in ¼ cup of cool, unchlorinated water (If you are using farm-fresh milk, you may omit this ingredient. Calcium chloride acts to firm up the curd of milk that has been homogenized because homogenization breaks down the fat globules in milk)

½ tsp powdered mesophilic starter (If you are using a prepared starter, use 4 ounces)

¼ tablet of vegetable rennet dissolved in ¼ cup of cool, unchlorinated water (If you are using liquid rennet, use ¼ tsp)

2 to 4 tbsp of heavy cream (optional)

Salt (optional)

Directions

1. Pour the milk in a stainless-steel pot.

2. Place the pot in a warm water bath and bring the temperature of the milk to 72°.

3. Stir the calcium chloride into the milk, making sure to mix it thoroughly.

4. Gently stir the mesophilic starter into the milk, making sure to mix it thoroughly.

5. Gently stir the rennet mixture into the milk, making sure to mix it thoroughly.

6. Cover the pot and let the mixture sit at room temperature for about six hours.

7. At this point, you should have a soft but firm curd that is about the consistency of custard. A knife inserted into the curd should produce a clean break. Likewise, you can test the consistency of the curd by inserting your

finger. *See instructions on cutting the curds in Chapter 10.* If the curd has not set to make a clean break, allow it to ripen for another hour or two.

8. Cut curds into ½-inch cubes.

9. Allow the curds to settle for 15 minutes. This allows for some of the whey to separate from the curds because the whey will rise to the top.

10. In a double boiler, very slowly heat the curds and whey to 110°. The temperature should increase from about 72° to 110° over a 45-minute period.

11. During the heating process, the curds should be stirred very gently every five minutes. Your goal with the stirring is to bring the curds that are on the bottom to the top as you evenly heat them.

12. Hold the temperature between 110° and 112° for 30 minutes.

13. As you heat the curds, you will notice that they are expelling more whey and are becoming firmer.

14. After 30 minutes, you can test the firmness of the curd by squeezing one in your fingers. If the curd feels mushy (like custard), you should continue to cook it a little more. Continue to occasionally give the curds a gentle stir, as well. If the curd feels somewhat firm, you are ready to move on.

15. Once you have a somewhat firm curd, remove the pot from the heat.

16. Allow the curds and whey to sit for about 15 minutes. The curds will settle to the bottom of the pot as the whey rises to the top.

17. Line a colander with a large, doubled piece of cheesecloth. Make sure the cloth is large enough that you will be able to bring the corners together in a bag for the cheese to drain. Place the colander over a pot to catch the whey.

18. Gently pour the curds into the cheesecloth-lined colander.

19. Allow curds to drain in colander for about ten minutes.

20. Bring and tie corners of cheesecloth together to form a bag.

21. Prepare a large pot of cold water.

22. After the bag of curds has drained for 15 minutes, dip the bag into the cold water.

23. Place the bag of curds back into the colander and allow it to drain for ten minutes.

24. Untie the bag and transfer the curds to a bowl.

25. By this point, the curds should be very firm.

26. Break the curds up by hand into smaller pieces. *See instructions for milling curds in Chapter 10.*

27. If you plan on adding salt, herbs, or spices to your cottage cheese, this is the time to do it.

28. Again, if you like a creamier cottage cheese, you can add cream when the cottage cheese is served, but do not add it until then, as the curds will soak up the cream, and the result will be a mess of matted curd.

Large-curd cottage cheese II

This cottage-cheese recipe varies from the previous recipe in that it does not call for a prepared starter but employs cultured buttermilk. Technically speaking, cultured buttermilk is the starter, and cultured buttermilk is made with a mesophilic starter. So, cultured buttermilk might be called your cottage cheese mother culture. The wonderful thing about using buttermilk as a starter in cheese recipes is it is much easier to access than direct-set mesophilic starters, especially if you already have a serial batch of cultured buttermilk in your refrigerator.

Ingredients

1 gallon milk (whole, low-fat, or skim)

¼ tablet of vegetable rennet dissolved in ¼ cup of cool, unchlorinated water (If you are using liquid rennet, use ¼ tsp)

¼ cup homemade cultured buttermilk (If you use store-bought buttermilk, make sure that you get the purest product you can buy. Many store-bought cultured buttermilks are filled with artificial flavorings, colors, and ingredients you may not want in your cottage cheese. Also, some of these ingredients may inhibit the coagulation of the milk)

Salt (to taste)

Directions

1. Pour the milk into a stainless-steel double-boiler pot.

2. Heat milk to 90°.

3. Add cultured buttermilk. Stir well.

4. Gently stir dissolved rennet mixture to the milk mixture.

5. Remove from heat and cover.

6. Allow mixture to sit at room temperature for about an hour.

7. Check the development of the curd.

8. If the curd has formed into a custard-like consistency, you are ready to proceed. If the curd has not quite formed, allow the mixture to sit for another 30 minutes.

9. Once the curd has formed, cut into 1-inch pieces.

10. Allow the curds to sit for 15 minutes.

11. In the double boiler, heat the curds very slowly to 110° over a 30-minute period.

12. As you heat the curds, very gently stir them to bring the curds on the bottom to the top. This allows the curds to be more evenly heated.

13. Stir every five minutes.

14. After the curd reaches 110°, hold that temperature for 20 to 30 minutes.

15. As you heat the curds, you will notice that they are expelling more whey and are becoming firmer.

16. After 20 minutes, you can test the firmness of the curd by squeezing one in your fingers. If the curd feels mushy (like custard), you should continue

to cook it a little more. Continue to occasionally give the curds a gentle stir as well. If the curd feels somewhat firm, you are ready to move on.

17. Once you have a somewhat firm curd, remove the pot from the heat.

18. Allow the curds and whey to sit for about 15 minutes. The curds will settle to the bottom of the pot as the whey rises to the top.

19. Line a colander with a large, doubled piece of cheesecloth. Make sure the cloth is large enough that you will be able to bring the corners together in a bag for the cheese to drain. Place the colander over a pot to catch the whey.

20. Gently pour the curds into the cheesecloth-lined colander.

21. Allow curds to drain in colander for about ten minutes.

22. Bring and tie corners of cheesecloth together to form a bag.

23. Prepare a large pot of cold water.

24. After the bag of curds has drained for 15 minutes, dip the bag into the cold water.

25. Place the bag of curds back into the colander and allow it to drain for ten minutes.

26. Untie the bag and transfer the curds to a bowl.

27. By this point, the curds should be very firm.

28. Break the curds up by hand into smaller pieces. *See instructions for milling curds in Chapter 10.*

29. If you plan on adding salt, herbs, or spices to your cottage cheese, this is the time to do it.

30. Again, if you like a creamier cottage cheese, you can add cream when the cottage cheese is served, but do not add it until then, as the curds will soak up the cream, and the result will be a mess of matted curd.

Temperature

Be sure to watch your temperature very closely in all of the cottage cheeses. It is vital that you do not allow the milk temperature to go over 120° because this will cause your starter, especially if you are using buttermilk or yogurt, to curdle as you add it to the milk.

Farmer's Cheese

Once you have made these basic cottage cheese recipes, you will want to expand your repertoire by branching out and making many more of the cheeses that belong to this particular line of the cheese family. Farmer's cheese is a variety of cheese that is very much like cottage cheese (especially if the farmer lives in a cottage), but there may be a few slight variations in procedure. This whole class of cheeses — including cottage cheese, farmer's cheese, pot cheese, and a few of the cheeses you made earlier (buttermilk cheese, yogurt cheese, and quark) — comprise aspects that are, indeed, all very similar in nature. If you go back and examine the ingredients and procedures for making each of cheeses, you may get confused as to which is cottage cheese, what is farmer's cheese, and what exactly pot cheese is. Not to worry; once you get the basics down, you will be coming up with your own variations on this fundamental farmer's cottage pot cheese.

In the meantime, here is another recipe for this timeless classic. This one will be called farmer's cheese.

Ingredients
1 gallon whole milk
1 cup room temperature plain homemade yogurt (can be low-fat)
¼ tablet of vegetable rennet dissolved in ¼ cup of cool, unchlorinated water
(If you are using liquid rennet, use ¼ tsp)
Salt (optional)

Directions

1. Pour the milk into a stainless-steel double-boiler pot.

2. Heat milk to 95°.

3. Add yogurt. Stir well.

4. Gently stir dissolved rennet mixture in the milk mixture.

5. Remove from heat and cover.

6. Allow mixture to sit at room temperature for about an hour.

7. Check the development of the curd.

8. If the curd has formed into a custard-like consistency, you are ready to proceed. If the curd has not quite formed, allow the mixture to sit for another 30 minutes.

9. Once the curd has formed, cut them into 1-inch pieces.

10. Allow the curds to sit for 15 minutes.

11. In the double boiler, heat the curds very slowly to 110°. You should allow the curds to reach 110° over a 30-minute period.

12. As you heat the curds, very gently stir them to bring the curds on the bottom to the top. This allows the curds to be more evenly heated.

13. Stir every five minutes.

14. After the curd reaches 110°, hold that temperature for 20 to 30 minutes.

15. As you heat the curds, you will notice that they are expelling more whey and becoming firmer.

16. Line a colander with a large, doubled piece of cheesecloth. Make sure the cloth is large enough that you will be able to bring the corners together in a bag for the cheese to drain. Place the colander over a pot to catch the whey.

17. Gently pour the curds into the cheesecloth-lined colander.

18. Allow curds to drain in colander for about an hour. At this point, the whey has probably stopped draining through the colander.

19. Transfer the cheese to a bowl and salt to taste.

20. If you salted the cheese, stir it well to evenly distribute salt.

21. Line two cheese molds with a double layer of cheesecloth. Make sure the cloth is large enough that you will be able to bring the corners together over the top of the filled molds.

22. Place the cheesecloth-lined molds in a pie plate or a similar dish that will be used to catch whey as it drains from the cheese.

23. Fill the cheesecloth-lined molds with the cheese.

24. Fold the cheesecloth over the top of the cheese and place 2 pounds of weight on top to press the cheese. A can of juice or a filled quart jar is a good weight to use for this purpose.

25. Place the cheese in the refrigerator and press for four hours.

26. Remove the cheese from the refrigerator and unwrap it from the cheese-cloth.

27. This cheese is best served fresh. It will keep in a closed container in the refrigerator for a week.

Pot Cheese

This can be considered one of the most basic cheese recipes for you to experiment with. There has been reference to simplicity along the way in this book and, by now, you have read the repeated story of the coagulated milk in the saddlebag. This recipe comes as close as possible to what that original cheese must have been like.

It is presumed that you do not have a saddlebag made from the second stomach of a cow as one of your standard kitchen utensils, but that does not matter here. What does matter for this recipe is that you have farm-fresh milk.

Like the other cheeses of this branch of the cheese family tree, there are many variations on this basic theme of what is considered pot cheese. Some will claim that the buttermilk cheese you made earlier is pot cheese. Some will offer up the fromage blanc recipe you made earlier as pot cheese. You may share this recipe with someone who will swear it is the Mexican queso blanco. Again, many of these names are interchangeable and will vary depending on whom you trade recipes and share cheese with.

The consistency of this cheese is similar in nature to cream cheese, and the taste is somewhat plain. The wonderful trait about this cheese is that it accepts the variety of flavors you can give it by introducing herbs, spices, and fruits.

What follows here is the most basic cheese recipe this book has to offer.

Ingredients
1 quart farm-fresh milk
Salt (optional)
Homemade butter (optional)

Directions
1. In a glass container, allow milk to ripen in a warm place, though out of the sun, for 24 hours. Room temperature or warmer — not hot — is fine for this.

2. Pour ripened milk into the stainless-steel pot of a double boiler.

3. Gently heat milk until the curds and whey separate.

4. Line a colander with a large, doubled piece of cheesecloth. Make sure the cloth is large enough that you will be able to bring the corners together in a bag for the cheese to drain. Place the colander over a pot to catch the whey.

5. Gently pour the curds into the cheesecloth-lined colander.

6. Allow curds to drain in colander for about ten minutes.

7. Bring and tie corners of cheesecloth together to form a bag.

8. Hang bag over pot for further draining.

9. Allow to drain for about four hours or until desired consistency is reached.

10. Salt to taste if desired.

11. Add butter and work it in with a wooden spoon if desired.

12. Can be refrigerated in a sealed container for up to a week.

Paneer (or Panir)

You may be thinking at this point that an entire book can be written about cottage cheese and its many cousins, and you are correct in your thinking. So, before this section takes over this entire book, one more recipe from this family tree will be offered before you move on to other areas.

Paneer is the Indian variety of soft cheese; you may have tasted paneer in Indian restaurants before. Also, as you read this recipe, you may think that you have seen it elsewhere in this book. However, look carefully at the differences in technique and ingredients as you compare this recipe with that of lemon cheese.

Ingredients
1 gallon whole milk
Juice of one lemon (Have a second lemon on hand)

Directions
1. Pour milk into a stainless-steel pot.

2. Stirring constantly over a direct heat, bring milk to a low boil.

3. Remove milk from heat and allow milk foam to subside slightly.

4. Squeeze lemon juice directly into the milk and stir.

5. Put the milk back on the heat and stir for about 30 seconds.

6. Remove milk from heat and continue to stir until curds form.

7. At this point, the whey should be somewhat clear as opposed to milky-looking. If your whey is still milky, return to heat and add the juice of another half lemon. Keep stirring.

8. Once you have definite curd and whey separation, remove the pot from the heat and allow it to sit undisturbed for 15 minutes.

9. As the curds and whey sit, the curds will fall to the bottom of the pan as the whey rises to the top.

10. Line a colander with a large, doubled piece of cheesecloth. Make sure the cloth is large enough that you will be able to bring the corners together in a bag for the cheese to drain. Place the colander over a pot to catch the whey.

11. Gently pour or ladle the curds into the cheesecloth-lined colander.

12. Allow curds to drain in colander for about ten minutes.

13. Bring and tie corners of cheesecloth together to form a bag.

14. Hang the bag above a pot to catch the whey.

15. Twist the bag several times to squeeze the cheese and force more whey from the bag.

16. Place the bag of cheese in the colander and place a plate on top of the bag.

17. Place a 5-pound weight (½-gallon milk bottle) on top of the plate to press the cheese.

18. Press cheese for one to two hours.

19. Unwrap the cheese from the cheesecloth.

20. This cheese is best served fresh. It will keep in a closed container in the refrigerator for a week.

Soft Cheese Serving Suggestions

Like any other cheese, if you have fresh homemade bread or crackers, you can enjoy the cheese with, all the better. While you will probably find that just about any kind of homemade bread will go well with this cheese, it is suggested that a good sourdough baguette or unleavened flatbread is the preferred cheese-delivery vehicle.

If you are reading this before you have made your cottage cheese, you may be wondering about enjoying cottage cheese on bread or crackers. But you will find that once you make this homemade version of cottage cheese, it is much more bread- and cracker-friendly than the overly creamy version of cottage cheese that you find in your grocery store dairy case because it will not be as runny.

A number of the recipes concluded with suggestions of adding herbs and spices. Because these cheeses are so mild, any herb or spice you add will give the cheese its own pronounced flavor. Herb suggestions for the cheeses listed in this chapter are chives, basil, dill, or parsley. If you have a garden and grow scallions or garlic, try adding these fresh chopped herbs to your cheese. You can also add a variety of spices to these cheeses to give them all a new taste. Try adding celery seed, freshly ground black pepper, chili pepper, or cayenne pepper.

Below are some wonderful recipes that show just how far you can go in developing recipes with any of the these farmer's, cottage, or pot cheeses. The following two recipes derive from Ethiopian cuisine, which is known for its spicy foods. If you have ever eaten at an Ethiopian restaurant, you know that you are often left without the traditional utensils of Western dining. Many of the dishes are made for and eaten with flat, unleavened bread, and this bread is employed as the primary utensil.

The first recipe here is for a dish known as Niter Kebbeh, or spiced butter. This recipe will remind you of the chapter on butter, as this is a recipe that produces a spiced, clarified butter.

This Niter Kebbeh is Ethiopian in origin, but it is a recipe that is quite commonly made throughout Northern Africa. It can be found in the dishes of Somalia, Eritrea, and Egypt.

Niter Kebbeh

Ingredients
1 pound homemade butter (unsalted)
2 tsp fresh, finely grated ginger root
1 tsp ground turmeric
$1/_8$ tsp ground cardamom seeds

1 cinnamon stick

Dash of freshly ground nutmeg

Dash of ground cloves

1 small, yellow onion, peeled and chopped very finely

2 cloves crushed garlic

Dash of cayenne pepper

Freshly ground black pepper to taste

Salt to taste

Directions

1. Measure out all of the spices prior to starting.

2. Melt butter in a heavy saucepan over low to moderate heat. Take care not to let the butter brown.

3. Allow the butter to boil and come to a foam.

4. Stir in all the remaining ingredients.

5. Lower heat and cook, uncovered and undisturbed, for 45 minutes.

6. At this point, you should have golden brown milk solids on the bottom of the pan and clear butter on the top.

7. Remove from heat.

8. Line a colander or small strainer with a doubled piece of cheesecloth. Place the strainer over a small bowl.

9. Slowly pour the liquid from the pan into the cheesecloth-lined strainer, taking care to try to only pour off the clarified butter from the top.

10. The liquid you pour off is the Niter Kebbeh. It can be kept in a sealed jar in your refrigerator for two months.

To use this delicious spiced butter with some of that wonderful soft cheese you have just made, use the following recipe.

Saharan Cheese

Ingredients

1 pound homemade cottage cheese, farmer's cheese, or pot cheese

3 tbsp Niter Kebbeh

Cayenne pepper to taste

Freshly ground black pepper to taste

Salt to taste

Directions

1. Gently stir Niter Kebbeh into cheese.
2. Add additional ingredients to taste.
3. Serve with flatbread.

Another way to enjoy any of these cheeses is with fresh fruit. They are especially good with apples, pears, figs, grapes, or raisins. Add nuts such as walnuts, pine nuts, or pecans to the fruit and cheese.

Some fruits work better with cottage cheese after you add a little cream to the cheese. Juicier fruits, such as peaches or berries of any kind, are delicious when mixed with cottage cheese and enough cream to give the dish a smoother texture. Here is a good example of a fruit salad that can be made with any of the soft farmer's, cottage, or pot cheeses.

Cottage Cheese Fruit Salad

Ingredients

½ cup honey

1 tsp grated lemon zest (Make sure to use only the zest and not the pith, which is the white substance between the peel and the fruit)

¼ cup freshly squeezed lemon juice

¼ tsp dry mustard

Pinch of salt

1 pound homemade cottage cheese, farmer's cheese, or pot cheese

½ **cup peeled and shredded carrots**

¼ **cup seedless raisins**

¼ **cup heavy cream** (optional)

Lettuce leaves

1 small melon of your choice, halved, seeded, peeled, and sliced into wedges

1 kiwi, pared and sliced

Assortment of seedless grape varieties

1 cup strawberries, sliced

Directions

1. For a dressing, whisk together honey, lemon zest, lemon juice, dry mustard, and salt.

2. Cover dressing and set aside. Do not refrigerate.

3. In a glass or food-grade plastic bowl, combine cheese, carrots, and raisins.

4. Cover fruit and cheese. Chill until ready to serve.

5. Just prior to serving, arrange a bed of lettuce on a serving plate.

6. If you desire a creamier cheese and fruit mixture, gently stir the cream into the cheese and fruit.

7. Spoon and arrange cheese and fruit mixture onto lettuce bed.

8. Arrange additional fruit around cheese.

9. Serve with zesty lemon-honey dressing.

Because these cheeses are so mild, they are perfect for experimenting with a wide variety of flavors and textures. They lend themselves perfectly to hours and years of kitchen play. Making and enjoying these cheeses is a great way to get kids involved and interested in the art and craft of making cheese. And again, because of the mild flavor of these cheeses, most kids will enjoy eating up their kitchen experiments. Can you flavor cottage cheese with chocolate syrup? Get the kids in the kitchen and give it a try.

Troubleshooting Soft Cheese

Because soft cheese is made with fairly simple principles, there is not much that can go wrong in making it. There are, however, a few things that you do need to watch out for.

If your milk is not coagulating and forms a curd:

- The rennet you used may have been bad. Rennet will last about two years in the freezer (if you are using rennet tablets). If you use liquid rennet, it can be refrigerated for about a year.

- Diluting it in warm water may have harmed the rennet. Take care that you dilute your rennet in water below 60°.

- You may have used too little rennet. Use the amount called for in the recipe.

If an overly soft curd has developed:

- You may have over-heated your milk. Take care to watch temperatures closely as you heat the milk.

- You may have used ultra-pasteurized milk. Check the milk's label before you start to make sure that you have the right milk.

If your milk coagulates immediately:

- The milk may have been overly acidic. The acidity of the milk increases as it ripens. Fresh milk will generally not have the problem of being overly acidic; however, milk that is past its prime could cause you problems in this area.

One final reminder about soft cheese (and cheese making and cooking in general) before you move on: Take notes. Do not be afraid to write in your cookbooks or even this book. Better yet, keep a cooking notebook handy to keep track of what you do and how you do it. The notes you take will help you to monitor your progress, make note of your successes, and correct your failures. You will have failures — we all do. You, too, will come up with your own solution. Take note of it. Besides, you will want to have a record of your successes when someone tastes one of your very own soft cheese creations and asks, "Can I have that recipe?"

CHAPTER 12

Making Italian Cheese

Italian cheese is a category all its own because it is a bridge between soft cheese and hard cheese. A number of the cheeses included in this category might well be referred to as semi-soft cheeses. Indeed, some recipes are very simple for making soft cheese (ricotta); some cheese is neither soft nor hard (semi-soft) and requires a technique that no other cheese requires (such as stretching Mozzarella cheese); and some Italian cheese is hard and requires aging for as long as a year (Parmesan).

Italian cheese is quite popular in the United States. You read earlier about the amount of Mozzarella sold in America, and that Mozzarella is quickly catching up with cheddar in popularity. This, no doubt, is due to the fact that Mozzarella is most people's favorite pizza cheese. There are several recipes for Mozzarella included in this chapter, and you can get kids involved in many of these recipes. Mozzarella is a cheese that needs to be kneaded and stretched to acquire its smooth consistency, so get the kids some clean rubber gloves and gather around the kitchen table for some Mozzarella stretching.

You will also get another opportunity to use your grill in this chapter because you will learn the technique of smoking cheese. Smoked Mozzarella cheese is known as scamorza, and you can smoke this cheese using your grill of a smoker.

You have read many times throughout this book that whey can be kept for a variety of uses. You will learn what could be the best of all possible uses of fresh whey when you learn how to make fresh ricotta cheese with the whey that is produced when you make Mozzarella cheese. Imagine a big dish of lasagna made with your fresh, homemade Mozzarella and ricotta cheeses. This will certainly make you ready to get back into the kitchen.

Mozzarella

The best place to begin learning how to make Italian cheese is with Mozzarella. Mozzarella is so popular because of its mild flavor and it meltability. It is an incredibly versatile cheese that can be a part of a number of baked dishes, from lasagna and pizza to macaroni and cheese and quiche.

Traditionally, Mozzarella is made with the milk of a water buffalo. The fancy cheese shops today sell Mozzarella made with the traditional ingredients. You can make Mozzarella with cow's milk (whole, low-fat, or skim), goat's milk, sheep's milk, or just about any kind of milk you might imagine, as long as you do not use ultra-pasteurized milk. It is recommended that as you learn to make Mozzarella, you use whole milk because it has a higher fat content than low-fat or skim milk, making the cheese more pliable in the stretching phase. The more pliable the cheese, the easier it is to learn the technique.

Included here are several variations on making this extremely versatile cheese. Like many other cheese recipes in this book, once you understand the basic process, you may come up with your own methods and recipes for producing Mozzarella cheese.

Practice
Mozzarella making is a technique that takes practice. Do not expect to make a fine Italian deli style of Mozzarella cheese on your first attempt. The process of making Mozzarella includes several different techniques that are quite different from any of the processes you have worked with to this point.

Be patient and have fun learning. The good news is that in most cases, even if your Mozzarella is not deli-suitable, it will still taste delicious; once you melt it in that lasagna, no one will know the difference.

Mozzarella I

This is perhaps the most basic of all the Mozzarella recipes because it calls for no starter culture and has very few ingredients. With one exception, the recipes that follow this one have the same basic techniques. The only Mozzarella recipe that is slightly different is the quick Mozzarella recipe (Mozzarella III) that is made using your microwave oven.

This recipe will yield about 1 pound of fresh Mozzarella.

Ingredients

1 gallon milk (For this particular recipe, whole milk is best, though you can use low-fat or skim)
1 ¼ tsp citric acid dissolved in ¼ cup of cool, unchlorinated water
¼ tablet of vegetable rennet dissolved in ¼ cup of cool, unchlorinated water
½ gallon hot water (110°)
¼ cup salt

Directions

1. Pour milk into the stainless-steel pot of a double boiler.

2. Slowly heat the milk to 90°.

3. Thoroughly whisk the citric acid solution into the milk.

4. Allow the milk to rest for 30 minutes at 90°.

5. Gently stir the rennet mixture to the milk, making sure to thoroughly mix.

6. Cover the pot and allow the milk to sit at 90° for 60 to 90 minutes.

7. After 60 minutes, check the curd for a yogurt-like consistency. Again, you are looking for a clean break in the curd when you insert a clean finger.

8. Very carefully cut the curd into ½-inch cubes. *Review the section on cutting curds in Chapter 10.*

9. Allow the curds 20 to 30 minutes to settle after you have initially cut them. The curds will slowly sink to the bottom of the pan and the whey will rise to the top.

10. While it is not absolutely necessary to check the pH level of the cheese at this point, if you have pH test strips, you should check levels now. Remove a little of whey from the pot and place it in a bowl. Dip the pH strips into the whey; the pH reading should be about 6.5. Remember, Mozzarella makers of old did not have pH test strips. You will probably be all right if you do not test, but it is interesting to note the changes in the acidity level of the liquid. The lower the pH number, the more acidic the liquid is. In the case of cheese making, you are trying to encourage the production of lactic acid. In making Mozzarella cheese, the recommended pH levels inform you when the cheese can be stretched, as the acidity level affects the consistency of the curd.

11. Begin to very slowly increase the heat of the curds and whey to 100°. You want to increase the heat of the curds and whey by about 2° every five minutes.

12. Gently stir the curds several times during this heating process to allow them to be more evenly heated. As the curds heat, they will expel more whey and become firmer.

13. When the temperature of the curds and whey reaches 100°, remove them from the double boiler.

14. Allow the curds and whey to sit undisturbed for ten minutes.

15. Line a colander with a large, doubled piece of cheesecloth. Place the colander over a pot to catch the whey.

16. Gently pour or ladle the curds into the cheesecloth-lined colander.

17. Allow curds to drain in colander for about five minutes.

18. Place the curds back in the pot they cooked in, and place that pot in a hot water bath. You can place the pot in a sink filled with 100° water.

19. The curds will continue to acidify and expel whey that will rise to the top.

20. Ladle the whey off of the curds every 20 to 30 minutes or so as you slowly turn over the mass of curd.

21. Keep the temperature of the water in the sink at about 100°, and continue the process of turning the curds and removing the whey for about two and a half hours.

22. If you are testing the pH level of the whey, this is a good time to check it again. After two and a half hours, the pH level should be 5.3.

23. After two and half hours (or when the pH level has reached 5.3), it is time to begin to work the curd.

24. Heat ½ gallon of water to 170°.

25. Add ¼ cup of salt to that water.

26. Working on a sterile cutting board, remove the mass of curd and take off two or three pieces that are about ½-inch.

27. Put the cubes in the hot water.

28. Wearing clean rubber gloves, knead the cubes between your fingers.

29. The cubes should melt together and become one shiny mass that will stretch as you work it.

30. Be sure that when you knead the cheese, you do so gently. If you handle it too roughly, you will work butterfat out of the curd, and you want to retain the butterfat.

31. Once you are able to knead the sample to be smooth and stretchable, repeat the process with the rest of the curds. Knead a small handful at

a time so the resulting mass of each bit worked is about the size of a tennis ball.

32. As you work the curds into the cheese, be patient. It takes about ten to 20 minutes of kneading each mass to achieve proper consistency.

33. You can dip the cheese in the hot water as you knead it to keep it pliable.

34. Ideally, your goal is to get your cheese to stretch like long, stretchy taffy.

35. The cheese you are not kneading should be on the cutting board. As you begin to work each small mass of cheese, move it to the hot water and then begin to knead it.

36. You will need to replenish your hot water regularly as you work to keep it hot.

37. As you finish kneading the cheese and it reaches a consistency you are happy with, place the cheese in cool water, allowing the cheese to firm up.

38. If you like your cheese somewhat salty, you can put the cheese in a cool brine solution to get firm. The brine can be made of ½ gallon of cool water and 2 cups of kosher salt.

39. Allow the cheese to rest in the brine for about an hour.

40. Remove the cheese from the brine and pat the cheese dry with a paper towel.

41. Cheese will keep for a week in a sealed container in the refrigerator.

42. Fresh Mozzarella can be frozen in a sealed container for up to three months.

Mozzarella II

Here is a variation on the recipe for basic Mozzarella cheese. As you learn how to make this cheese, you will discover there are many variations on the basic processes for making this popular semi-soft cheese. The more experienced you become, the more you can begin to experiment with various types of milk. Here again, as a novice cheese maker, you should proceed with whole cow's milk. However, as you become more experienced, you can make this recipe with low-fat or skim milk, as well as goat's milk or any kind of milk you choose, as long as it is not ultra-pasteurized.

Note: This is the first cheese recipe in this book that calls for a thermophilic culture. *See notes on thermophilic culture in Chapter 2.*

Ingredients
1 gallon whole milk
½ tsp powdered thermophilic culture (If using a prepared culture, use 4 ounces)
¼ tablet vegetable rennet dissolved in ¼ cup cool, unchlorinated water (If using liquid rennet, use ¼ tsp)
1 pound cheese salt (for brine solution)
½ gallon cold water (for brine solution)

Directions
1. Pour milk into the stainless-steel pot of a double boiler.

2. Slowly heat the milk to 90°.

3. Gently stir the thermophilic culture into the milk.

4. Allow the milk to ripen for 45 minutes at 90°.

5. Gently stir the rennet mixture to the milk, making sure to thoroughly mix for ten minutes.

6. Cover the pot and allow the milk to sit at 90° for 60 to 90 minutes.

7. After 60 minutes, check the curd for a yogurt-like consistency. Again, you are looking for a clean break in the curd when you insert a clean finger.

8. Very carefully cut the curd into ½-inch cubes. *Review the section on cutting curds in Chapter 10.*

9. Allow the curds 20 to 30 minutes to settle at 90° after you have initially cut them. The curds will slowly sink to the bottom of the pan as the whey rises to the top.

10. Though it is not absolutely necessary to check the pH level of the cheese at this point, if you have pH test strips, you should check levels now. Remove a little whey from the pot and place it in a bowl. Dip the pH strips into the whey. The pH reading should be about 6.5. This tells you that the milk is becoming more acidic. Remember, Mozzarella makers of old did not have pH test strips. You will probably be all right if you do not test, but it is interesting to note the changes in the acidity level of the liquid.

11. Begin to very slowly increase the heat of the curds and whey to 105°. You want to increase the heat of the curds and whey by about 2° every five minutes.

12. Gently stir the curds several times during this heating process to allow them to be more evenly heated. As the curds heat, they will expel more whey and become firmer.

13. When the temperature of the curds and whey reaches 105°, allow them to cook at this temperature for ten minutes.

14. Remove the pot containing the curds and whey from the double boiler.

15. Allow the curds and whey to sit undisturbed for ten minutes.

16. Line a colander with a large, doubled piece of cheesecloth. Place the colander over a pot to catch the whey.

17. Gently pour or ladle the curds into the cheesecloth-lined colander.

18. Allow curds to drain in colander for about five minutes.

19. Place the curds back in the pot they cooked in, and place that pot back into the double boiler.

20. Reheat the curds to 105°.

21. The curds will continue to acidify and expel whey that will rise to the top.

22. Ladle the whey off the curds every 20 to 30 minutes as you slowly turn over the mass of curd.

23. Keep the temperature of the curds at 105° and continue the process of turning the curds and removing the whey for about two and a half hours.

24. If you are testing the pH level of the whey, this is a good time to check it again. After two and a half hours, the pH level should be 5.3.

25. After two and half hours (or when the pH level has reached 5.3), it is time to begin to work the curd.

26. Heat ½ gallon of water to 170°.

27. Add ¼ cup of salt to that water.

28. Working on a sterile cutting board, remove the mass of curd and take off two or three pieces that are about ½-inch.

29. Put the cubes in the hot water.

30. Wearing clean rubber gloves, knead the cubes between your fingers.

31. The cubes should melt together and become one shiny mass that will stretch as you work it.

32. Be sure that when you knead the cheese, you do so gently. If you handle it too roughly, you will work butterfat out of the curd, and you want to retain that fat.

33. Once you are able to knead the sample to be smooth and stretchable, repeat the process with the rest of the curds. Knead a small handful at a time so the resulting mass of each bit worked is about the size of a tennis ball.

34. As you work the curds into the cheese, be patient. It takes about ten to 20 minutes of kneading each mass to achieve proper consistency.

35. You can dip the cheese in the hot water as you knead it to keep it pliable.

36. Ideally, your goal is to get your cheese to stretch like long, stretchy taffy.

37. The cheese you are not kneading should be on the cutting board. As you begin to work each small mass of cheese, move it to the hot water and then begin to knead it.

38. You will need to replenish your hot water regularly as you work to keep it hot.

39. As you finish kneading the cheese and it reaches a consistency you are happy with, place the cheese in cool water, allowing the cheese to firm up.

40. If you like your cheese somewhat salty, you can put the cheese in a cool brine solution to get firm. The brine can be made of ½ gallon of cool water and 2 cups of kosher salt.

41. Allow the cheese to rest in the brine for about an hour.

42. Pat the cheese dry with paper towel.

43. Cheese will keep for a week in a sealed container in the refrigerator.

44. Fresh Mozzarella can be frozen in a sealed container for up to three months.

Mozzarella III

If you are new to Mozzarella making, this recipe will be a big surprise to you. You can make fresh Mozzarella cheese in your microwave oven in about half an hour, and it tastes wonderful.

As in making the first two Mozzarella recipes, this one takes a bit of practice. Once you get the hang of it, though, you will love the product enough to try it again and again.

Ingredients

1 gallon milk (You can use whole or low-fat)

2 tsp powdered citric acid dissolved in ½ cup cool water

¼ tablet vegetable rennet dissolved in ¼ cup cool, unchlorinated water (If using liquid rennet, use ¼ tsp)

Salt (to taste)

Directions

1. Pour milk into the stainless-steel pot of a double boiler.

2. Add the citric acid solution to the milk while it is still cold (50° to 55°).

3. Stir well.

4. Slowly heat the milk to 100°.

5. You will notice that the milk is starting to curdle.

6. Gently stir in the rennet solution and stir well.

7. Allow the milk to heat to 105°.

8. When the milk gets to 105°, remove the pot from the double boiler and the heat.

9. Cover the milk and allow it to sit for 15 minutes. You will notice that the curds have separated from the whey. The whey should be clear. If it is still a little milky-white, allow the mixture to sit a bit longer.

10. Use a large, shallow ladle to scoop the curds out of the pot and place them in a microwave-safe bowl. A 2-quart glass is preferred.

11. After you have transferred all the curd into the bowl, gently pour off any excess whey that may have been expelled while you were transferring the curd.

12. Place the bowl of curds in the microwave and microwave them on high for one minute.

13. Gently pour off any excess whey that was expelled as you heated the curds.

14. The curds will be hot. Wearing clean rubber gloves, gently knead the curds by folding them over back-to-front and side-to-side (as if you are kneading bread dough).

15. Place the bowl of curds back in the microwave on high for 30 seconds.

16. Gently pour off any excess whey that was expelled as you heated the curds.

17. Add salt to taste.

18. Gently knead the curds again by folding them over back-to-front and side-to-side.

19. Repeat the process of heating for 30 seconds, pouring off whey and gently kneading. The kneading helps to evenly heat the cheese.

20. Each time you heat the cheese, you will notice that it is growing more and more elastic.

21. As you knead, test the cheese by stretching it. If it breaks, you will need to heat it again. If the cheese stretches like taffy, it is finished.

22. When it is heated to the point of being very smooth and elastic, form the cheese into tennis-sized balls.

23. You can eat the Mozzarella warm, or you can drop them into a bowl of cold water to cool them down.

24. This cheese is best served very fresh and has a very short shelf life. It will keep in a sealed container in the refrigerator for about four days.

Grating Fresh Mozzarella

You might find that fresh Mozzarella is too moist to grate without making a big, sticky mess. If you would like to grate Mozzarella for use on pizza, put it in the freezer for about 30 minutes before grating. After that, it should be firm enough to stand up to the grater.

Making fresh Mozzarella cheese is another one of the moderately easy processes that, once you get the hang of it, can be adapted and experimented with to make an endless number of variations and forms. The recipes above instructed you to form the Mozzarella into balls, but you can just as easily form Mozzarella sticks. Mozzarella is also occasionally found braided. To do this, divide your still-hot Mozzarella into three parts and shape the parts into three fat "ropes," 12 to 18 inches long. While still hot, braid the ropes. After braiding, put the cheese into cold water to firm it up.

Scamorza

Scamorza is another cheese, like Mozzarella, that is known as a pasta filata-type cheese. Pasta filata translates literally to "spun paste." After making Mozzarella, you know exactly why this term is used. The name "scamorza" refers to cutting off a head in Italian. The shape of the cheese and the fact that you slice the cheese at the "neck" when you first eat it lends this cheese its gory name.

You will note that the ingredients of scamorza are exactly the same as those of the Mozzarella II recipe. Note, however, the slight differences in how the cheese is produced.

Later in this recipe, you will learn to smoke this cheese. Smoking is the most popular way that this mild cheese is eaten.

Ingredients

1 gallon whole milk

½ tsp powdered thermophilic culture (If using a prepared culture, use 4 ounces)

¼ tablet vegetable rennet dissolved in ¼ cup cool, unchlorinated water (If using liquid rennet, use ¼ tsp)

1 pound cheese salt (for brine solution)

½ gallon cold water (for brine solution)

Directions

1. Pour milk into the stainless-steel pot of a double boiler.

2. Slowly heat the milk to 97°.

3. Gently stir the thermophilic culture into the milk.

4. Allow the milk to ripen for 45 minutes at 97°.

5. Gently stir the rennet mixture into the milk, making sure to thoroughly mix for ten minutes.

6. Cover the pot and allow the milk to sit at 97° for 45 to 90 minutes.

7. After 45 minutes, check the curd for a yogurt-like consistency. Again, you are looking for a clean break in the curd when you insert a clean finger.

8. Very carefully cut the curd into ½-inch cubes. *Review the section on cutting curds in Chapter 10.*

9. Allow the curds 20 to 30 minutes to settle at 97° after you have initially cut them. The curds will slowly sink to the bottom of the pan as the whey rises to the top.

10. Although it is not absolutely necessary to check the pH level of the cheese at this point, if you have pH test strips, you should check levels now. Remove a little whey from the pot and place it in a bowl. Dip the pH strips into the whey. The pH reading should be about 6.5.

11. Begin to very slowly increase the heat of the curds and whey to 108°. You want to increase the heat of the curds and whey by about 2° every five minutes.

12. Gently stir the curds several times during this heating process. You will stir the curds to allow them to be more evenly heated. As the curds heat, they will expel more whey and become firmer.

13. When the temperature of the curds and whey reaches 108°, allow the curds and whey to cook at this temperature for ten minutes.

14. Remove the pot containing the curds and whey from the double boiler.

15. Allow the curds and whey to sit undisturbed for ten minutes.

16. Line a colander with a large, doubled piece of cheesecloth. Place the colander over a pot to catch the whey.

17. Gently pour or ladle the curds into the cheesecloth-lined colander.

18. Allow curds to drain in colander for about five minutes.

19. Place the curds back in the pot they cooked in and place that pot back into the double boiler.

20. Reheat the curds to 108°.

21. The curds will continue to acidify and expel whey that will rise to the top.

22. Ladle the whey off the curds every 20 to 30 minutes as you slowly turn over the mass of curd.

23. Keep the temperature of the curds at 105° and continue the process of turning the curds and removing the whey for about two and a half hours.

24. If you are testing the pH level of the whey, this is a good time to check it again. After two and a half hours, the pH level should be 5.3.

25. After two and half hours (or when the pH level has reached 5.3), it is time to begin to work the curd.

26. Heat ½ gallon of water to 170°.

27. Add ¼ cup of salt to that water.

28. Working on a sterile cutting board, remove the mass of curd and take off two or three pieces that are about ½-inch big.

29. Put the cubes in the hot water.

30. Wearing clean rubber gloves, knead the cubes between your fingers.

31. The cubes should melt together and become one shiny mass that will stretch as you work it.

32. Be sure that when you knead the cheese, you do so gently. If you handle it too roughly, you will work butterfat out of the curd, and you want to retain that fat.

33. Once you are able to knead the sample to be smooth and stretchable, repeat the process with the rest of the curds. Knead a small handful at a time so the resulting mass of each bit worked is about the size and shape of a large pear.

34. As you work the curds into the cheese, be patient. It takes about ten to 20 minutes of kneading each mass to achieve proper consistency.

35. You can dip the cheese in the hot water as you knead it to keep it pliable.

36. Ideally, your goal is to get your cheese to stretch like long, stretchy taffy.

37. The cheese you are not kneading should be on the cutting board. As you begin to work each small mass of cheese, move it to the hot water and then begin to knead it.

38. You will need to replenish your hot water regularly as you work to keep it hot.

39. As you finish kneading the cheese and it reaches a consistency you are happy with, place the cheese in cool water, allowing the cheese to firm up.

40. If you like your cheese somewhat salty, you can put the cheese in a cool brine solution to get firm. The brine can be made from ½ gallon of cool water and 2 cups of kosher salt.

41. Allow the cheese to rest in the brine for about an hour.

42. Take the cheese out of the brine and pat the cheese dry with a paper towel.

43. Tie kitchen twine around the pear-shaped cheese. Usually the twine will connect two cheese "pears" to be hung to ripen.

44. Hang the cheese to ripen at 50° and 85 percent humidity for three weeks.

45. You can get a sharper cheese by aging the cheese at 45° for two to 12 months.

Scamorza can be enjoyed in a number of ways. You can eat it fresh, as soon as it is made, as you would fresh Mozzarella, or you can eat it after aging it; it will have a decidedly sharper flavor. However, the most popular way to enjoy this cheese is scamorza "affumicata," or smoked.

In Chapter 11, you learned how to make the Finnish Leipäjuusto that called for you to broil or grill your soft cheese. Scamorza affumicata is another cheese that is produced by using a grill or smoker.

Scamorza appears here following the Mozzarella recipes because it is very much like Mozzarella, and you may smoke your Mozzarella in the same manner that you will smoke the scamorza. In fact, if you were to search for a variety of scamorza-making techniques, you are sure to find some that instruct you to simply smoke Mozzarella.

You can experiment by following these directions using any semi-soft cheese. The recipe for provolone that follows this recipe for scamorza is another semi-soft cheese that is frequently smoked.

Ingredients

Grill (A kettle grill with lid and an indirect source of heat works best. Indirect heating on a grill means that you will never have any part of the food you are cooking directly over the heat source. In smoking your cheese, you will use such a small amount of smoke material that you will have very little problem arranging your grill to accomplish this task)

Smoke material (This, like adding salt, herbs, or seasonings, is a matter of taste. You can purchase various types of smoke chips such as hickory, mesquite, pecan shells, or applewood in most locations where you purchase charcoal for grills. The smoke type you choose will be determined by your tastes and experimentation)

Scamorza (or any semi-soft cheese)

Cheesecloth

Mesh screen (Make sure it is a metal screen, not a plastic screen that will melt)

Oven thermometer (This item, while not absolutely necessary, will help you to keep an eye on the temperature of the grill)

Directions

1. The key is to use a small amount of smoke material. Your goal is to slightly dampen to the smoke material so it will produce a lot of smoke and very little heat.

2. Light three or four charcoal pieces.

3. Place the charcoal on top of the hickory, mesquite, pecan shells, or applewood to create a good amount of smoke without too much heat.

4. On the grill surface, above the coals, place two empty pans. One pan will used for water later on. Place this pan directly over the coals. Place your thermometer in the other.

5. Wrap the scamorza in cheesecloth.

6. Place the wrapped scamorza on the mesh screen.

7. Cover the grill with all of the vents open all the way. Ideally, you want to place the cover on the grill so that you can see the reading on the thermometer through an open vent.

8. Try not to let the temperature in the grill rise above 90°.

9. From here on, the amount of time you smoke your cheese is a judgment call. Smoke to taste. You can smoke the cheese anywhere from 30 minutes to eight hours. It is suggested that you begin by smoking cheese for a short period of time and experiment with the timing after your first or second forays into this process.

10. If the temperature rises above 90°, open the grill for a second or two to allow some heat to escape.

11. You can place one or two ice cubes in the empty water pan to bring the temperature down. This may cause condensation to form and drip onto your cheese or the coals. If it drips on the coals, it will produce more smoke.

12. If the condensation drips on your cheese, or if you find that your cheese starts to sweat, blot the moisture off with a paper towel.

13. Another way to bring the heat down and add smoke is to remove a burning piece of smoke chip and replace it with an unlit piece.

14. After you remove the cheese from the grill, allow it to cool completely prior to serving.

Provolone

Provolone is a cheese that is very similar to Mozzarella and scamorza in that provolone is a pasta filata, which is Italian for "spun paste." The primary difference between provolone and Mozzarella is that Mozzarella is made to be eaten fresh, while provolone is meant to be aged. Also, Mozzarella is considered to be a mild cheese, while provolone is somewhat sharper. Note the ingredient lipase powder in this recipe.

Ingredients

1 gallon whole milk

½ tsp powdered thermophilic culture (If using a prepared culture, use 4 ounces)

¼ tsp lipase powder dissolved in ¼ cup cool, unchlorinated water

½ tablet vegetable rennet dissolved in ¼ cup cool, unchlorinated water (If using liquid rennet, use ¼ tsp)

1 pound cheese salt (for brine solution)

½ gallon cold water (for brine solution)

Directions

1. Pour milk into the stainless-steel pot of a double boiler.

2. Slowly heat the milk to 97°.

3. Gently stir the thermophilic culture into the milk.

4. Allow the milk to ripen for an hour at 97°.

5. Add lipase solution and mix in thoroughly.

6. Allow milk to sit for 15 minutes.

7. Gently stir the rennet mixture to the milk, making sure to thoroughly mix for ten minutes.

8. Cover the pot and allow the milk to sit at 97° for 20 to 30 minutes.

9. After 20 minutes, check the curd for a yogurt-like consistency. Again, you are looking for a clean break in the curd when you insert a clean finger.

10. Very carefully cut the curd into ½-inch cubes. *Review the section on cutting curds in Chapter 10.*

11. Allow the curds 20 to 30 minutes to settle at 97° after you have initially cut them. The curds will slowly sink to the bottom of the pan, and the whey will rise to the top.

12. While it is not absolutely necessary to check the pH level of the cheese at this point, if you have pH test strips, check levels now. Remove a little whey from the pot and place it in a bowl. Dip the pH strips into the whey. The pH reading should be about 6.5.

13. Begin to very slowly increase the heat of the curds and whey to 140°. You want to increase the heat of the curds and whey by about 2° every five minutes.

14. Gently stir the curds several times during this process to allow them to be more evenly heated. As the curds heat, they will expel more whey and become firmer.

15. When the temperature of the curds and whey reaches 140°, allow them to cook at this temperature for five minutes.

16. Remove the pot containing the curds and whey from the double boiler.

17. Allow the curds and whey to sit undisturbed for 15 minutes.

18. Line a colander with a large, doubled piece of cheesecloth. Place the colander over a pot to catch the whey.

19. Gently pour or ladle the curds into the cheesecloth-lined colander.

20. Allow curds to drain in colander for about 30 minutes. While the curds are draining, keep them at about 108°. You can do this by putting a cover on the colander and placing the colander over the pot of hot whey.

21. Heat ½ gallon of water to 170° and pour it into a bowl.

22. Add ½ cup of salt to that water.

23. After 30 minutes, test the texture of a piece of curd. Wearing clean rubber gloves, dip a small piece of the curd into the bowl of hot water. Try to stretch it. If it stretches, you can proceed. If it does not stretch, wait 15 minutes and try again.

24. It could take as long as two hours for the cheese to ripen to the proper texture.

25. Working on a sterile cutting board, remove the mass of curd and take off two or three pieces that are about ½-inch long.

26. Put the cubes in the hot water.

27. Wearing clean rubber gloves, knead the cubes between your fingers.

28. The pieces should melt together and become one shiny mass that will stretch as you work it.

29. Be sure that when you knead the cheese, you do so gently. If you handle it too roughly, you will work butterfat out of the curd, and you want to retain that fat.

30. Once you are able to knead the sample to be smooth and stretchable, repeat the process with the rest of the curds. Knead a small handful at a time so the resulting mass of each bit worked is about the size and shape of a large pear.

31. As you work the curds into the cheese, be patient. It takes about ten to 20 minutes of kneading each mass to achieve proper consistency.

32. You can dip the cheese in the hot water as you knead it to keep it pliable.

33. Ideally, your goal is to get your cheese to stretch like long, stretchy taffy.

34. The cheese you are not kneading should be on the cutting board. As you begin to work each small mass of cheese, move it to the hot water and then begin to knead it.

35. You will need to replenish your hot water regularly as you work to keep it hot.

36. As you finish kneading the cheese and it reaches a consistency you are happy with, place the cheese in cool water, allowing the cheese to firm up.

37. If you like your cheese somewhat salty, you can put the cheese in a cool brine solution to get firm. The brine can be made of ½ gallon of cool water and 2 cups of kosher salt.

38. Allow the cheese to rest in the brine for about an hour.

39. Pat the cheese dry with a paper towel.

40. Tie kitchen twine around the pear-shaped cheese. Usually the twine will connect two cheese "pears" to be hung to ripen.

41. Hang the cheese to ripen at 50° and 85 percent humidity for three weeks.

42. You can get a sharper cheese by aging the cheese at 45° for two to 12 months.

43. This is another cheese that is often smoked. This cheese is good to smoke before aging. Follow the directions for smoking that appear prior to this recipe before hanging it to age.

The next two recipes in this chapter on Italian cheese are Romano and Parmesan. You will find that both cheeses have similar ingredients and processes used to produce these hard, aged, and sharp-flavored favorites.

Romano

Romano cheese is known as one of the world's oldest cheeses among cheese enthusiasts. There is evidence that Pecorino Romano (sheep's milk cheese) has been produced outside Rome since the 1st century AD. You have read several times already about the fateful camel with the saddlebags filled with milk. The original name of Romano cheese was "horseback cheese" ("caciocavallo" in Italian), for much the same reason.

Ingredients

2 gallons of low-fat milk
1 tsp thermophilic starter powder (If using a prepared culture, use ¼ cup)
¼ tsp lipase powder dissolved in ¼ cup cool, unchlorinated water

¼ tablet vegetable rennet dissolved in ¼ cup cool, unchlorinated water (If using liquid rennet, use ¼ tsp)
1 pound cheese salt (for brine solution)
½ gallon cold water (for brine solution)
Olive oil

Directions

1. Pour milk into the stainless-steel pot of a double boiler.

2. Slowly heat the milk to 90°.

3. Gently stir the thermophilic culture into the milk.

4. Allow the milk to ripen for an hour at 90°.

5. Add lipase solution and mix in thoroughly.

6. Allow milk to sit for 15 minutes.

7. Gently stir the rennet mixture into the milk, making sure to thoroughly mix for ten minutes.

8. Cover the pot and allow the milk to sit at 90° for 20 to 30 minutes.

9. After 20 minutes, check the curd for a yogurt-like consistency. Again, you are looking for a clean break in the curd when you insert a clean finger.

10. Very carefully cut the curd into ¼-inch cubes. *Review the section on cutting curds in Chapter 10.*

11. Begin to very slowly increase the heat of the curds and whey to 115°. You want to increase the heat of the curds and whey by about 2° every five minutes.

12. Hold the curds at 115° for 30 minutes. At this point, the curds should be firm enough to hold their shape when you gently squeeze them.

13. Line a colander with a large, doubled piece of cheesecloth. Place the colander over a pot to catch the whey.

14. Gently pour or ladle the curds into the cheesecloth-lined colander.

15. Line a cheese mold with cheesecloth.

16. Place the cheese mold in a pan to catch the draining whey.

17. Transfer the curds from the colander into the cheese mold.

18. Fold the cheesecloth over the top to the cheese curd.

19. Press the curds with 5 pounds of weight for 20 minutes.

20. Remove the cheese from the mold and unwrap the cheesecloth.

21. Flip the cheese over and re-wrap in the cheesecloth.

22. Place the cheesecloth-wrapped cheese back in the mold and press it at 10 pounds for 30 minutes.

23. Repeat the unwrapping, flipping, and rewrapping of the cheese.

24. Press at 20 pounds for three hours.

25. Repeat the unwrapping, flipping, and rewrapping of the cheese.

26. Press at 35 to 40 pounds for 12 hours.

27. Dissolve the cheese salt in the cold water to make a brine solution.

28. Unwrap the cheese and soak in the brine in the refrigerator for 12 hours.

29. While the cheese is soaking in the brine, flip it over every three to four hours.

30. Take the cheese out of the brine and pat dry with a paper towel.

31. Age the cheese at 55° and a relative humidity of 80 to 85 percent for three months to a year.

32. During the first four weeks of aging, you should turn the cheese over daily.

33. After a month, turn the cheese over once a week.

34. If mold forms on the cheese during the aging process, you can wipe it off with a clean cloth dampened with brine solution.

35. After aging for two months, you can lightly coat the outside of the cheese with olive oil.

36. The olive oil can be lightly applied on a monthly basis.

Parmesan

One of the most common cheeses served in the United States is Parmesan. Used most often as a condiment to top pasta dishes, pizza, and salad, Parmesan is a sharp-flavored grating cheese; that is, its texture and moisture content are such that it can be easily grated for use in various recipes. Parmesan is also one of the prime ingredients of pesto. The best Parmesan is aged for at least ten months.

Ingredients

1 gallon of low-fat cow's milk

1 gallon goat's milk (Note that you can make this cheese using only cow's milk, too. If you do, use the lipase powder listed below. No lipase is necessary if you combine the cow's and goat's milk)

1 tsp thermophilic starter powder (If using a prepared culture, use ¼ cup)

¼ tsp lipase powder dissolved in ¼ cup cool, unchlorinated water (See note about usage with milk above)

¼ tablet vegetable rennet dissolved in ¼ cup cool, unchlorinated water (If using liquid rennet, use ¼ tsp)

1 pound cheese salt (for brine solution)

½ gallon cold water (for brine solution)

Olive oil

Directions

1. Pour milk(s) into the stainless-steel pot of a double boiler.

2. Slowly heat the milk to 90°.

3. Gently stir the thermophilic culture into the milk.

4. Allow the milk to ripen for an hour at 90°.

5. Add lipase solution if you use only cow's milk; mix in thoroughly.

6. Allow milk to sit for 15 minutes.

7. Gently stir the rennet mixture into the milk, making sure to thoroughly mix for ten minutes.

8. Cover the pot and allow the milk to sit at 90° for 20 to 30 minutes.

9. After 20 minutes, check the curd for a yogurt-like consistency. Again, you are looking for a clean break in the curd when you insert a clean finger.

10. Very carefully cut the curd into ¼-inch cubes. *Review the section on cutting curds in Chapter 10.*

11. Begin to very slowly increase the heat of the curds and whey to 100°. You want to increase the heat of the curds and whey by about 2° every five minutes.

12. Gently stir the curds as you heat.

13. Very slowly increase the heat of the curds and whey to 125°, increasing by about 3° every five minutes.

14. At this point, the curds will have the appearance of large-grain rice and will have something of a squeak when you chew them.

15. Remove the pot of curds from the heat.

16. Allow the pot of curds to rest for five minutes.

17. Line a colander with a large, doubled piece of cheesecloth. Place the colander over a pot to catch the whey.

18. Gently pour or ladle the curds into the cheesecloth-lined colander.

19. Line a cheese mold with cheesecloth.

20. Place the cheese mold in a pan to catch the draining whey.

21. Transfer the curds from the colander into the cheese mold.

22. Fold the cheesecloth over the top to the cheese curd.

23. Press the curds with 5 pounds of weight for 20 minutes.

24. Remove the cheese from the mold and unwrap the cheesecloth.

25. Flip the cheese over and rewrap in the cheesecloth.

26. Place the cheesecloth-wrapped cheese back in the mold and press it at 10 pounds for 30 minutes.

27. Repeat the unwrapping, flipping, and rewrapping of the cheese.

28. Press at 15 pounds for three hours.

29. Repeat the unwrapping, flipping, and rewrapping of the cheese.

30. Press at 20 pounds for 12 hours.

31. Dissolve the cheese salt in the cold water to make a brine solution.

32. Unwrap the cheese and soak in the brine at room temperature for 24 hours.

33. While the cheese is soaking in the brine, flip it over every three to four hours.

34. Take the cheese out of the brine and pat dry with a paper towel.

35. Age the cheese at 55° and a relative humidity of 80 to 85 percent for at least ten months.

36. During the first four weeks of aging, you should turn the cheese over daily.

37. After a month, turn the cheese over once a week.

38. If mold forms on the cheese during the aging process, you can wipe it off with a clean cloth, dampened with brine solution.

39. After the cheese has been aging for two months, you can lightly coat the outside of the cheese with olive oil.

40. The olive oil can be lightly applied on a monthly basis.

Troubleshooting Italian Cheese

Some of these problems are particular to Italian cheese, but you will also find some fixes here for other types of cheeses.

If your curds will not come together:

- Make sure that your milk is not ultra-pasteurized. If your milk is not ultra-pasteurized and your curds have not come together, you should simply change the brand of milk you are using. This problem is often caused by how the milk was treated at the factory where it was processed.

If your cheese is bland and flavorless:

- You may consider using lipase powder if you have not used it. *Read about lipase powder in Chapter 2 of this book.*

- You may not have aged your cheese long enough. Be patient and try to age your cheese for at least the minimum time suggested in the recipe.

- You may not have allowed the starter to ripen the proper amount of time when you were making the cheese. When the starter is not allowed to ripen, the proper amount of acidity cannot be produced, and it is the acidity that gives the cheese much of its flavor. Likewise, overly ripened cheese becomes overly acidic and affects the cheese in quite the opposite way, making the cheese taste too strong.

If your cheese is extremely difficult to remove from the mold after pressing:

- The milk and/or the curd may have been contaminated during the cheese-making process. A bacteria or yeast contamination of the milk will cause a gas that expands the cheese during the pressing, making it difficult to extract from the mold. This is usually caused by a lack of cleanliness. Be sure to sterilize all your utensils prior to making cheese, and ensure your milk is fresh and cold before you start.

There is a good number of recipes in Chapter 16 that utilize one or more of these wonderful Italian cheeses. Whether you choose to astonish your friends and family with a pizza made with your own homemade Mozzarella and Parmesan, or experiment and entertain your guests with a stuffed Mozzarella appetizer, you are sure to please the palates of all those who are fortunate enough to come to the table. Have fun. *Buon appetito!*

CHAPTER 13

Whey Cheese

The first time you make a whey cheese, you will be struck by how easy and magical it is. Here is where you can make some use of all that whey you have been instructed to save in the many recipes that have come in the earlier chapters of this book. There are a number of other uses for the whey, but making more cheese is probably the best use of this cheese making by-product.

Ricotta

There are many ways to produce ricotta cheese. Some might tell you that the use of the word "cheese" to describe ricotta is not quite correct. Purists might tell you that ricotta is more of creamery product, much the same way sour cream or buttermilk is. The word "ricotta" means "re-cooked" in Italian and refers to the way that ricotta is made by re-cooking the whey that is produced in the making of other cheese.

Here is where we will split hairs. Cheese purists and the Food and Agriculture Organization of the United Nations will tell you that true cheese is the "fresh or matured product obtained by the drainage (of liquid) after the coagulation of milk, cream, skimmed or partly-skimmed milk, buttermilk, or combination thereof."

Furthermore, it is suggested that true cheese is the combination of dairy products (milk, cream, buttermilk, and so on) coagulated with rennet and an acid.

Given the above definition, ricotta is not a cheese. Whey ricotta, however, is the by-product of cheese production and, in most cheese-making directories, cheese shops, and grocery stores, you can find directions for making and buying ricotta cheese.

Several recipes for ricotta are offered here. Though this chapter covers whey cheeses, not all ricotta recipes are produced using whey. The recipes for ricotta are collected here together for your convenience.

Whey Ricotta

Originally, ricotta was produced from the whey by-product of Romano cheese. Cheese makers in Rome found that they had excessive amounts of whey that they could not dispose of by pouring it down the drain because whey produces something of an environmental problem: Whey is rich in protein and enzymes, thus it promotes the growth of algae in local water systems, rivers, and lakes. This overgrowth of algae depletes the oxygen in the water and kills fish. Something had to be done with the whey.

It was discovered that when the whey is reheated and a small amount of an acid is added to it (the amount of acid added depends on the amount of whey that is being reheated), the casein (milk protein) particles that remained in the liquid came together and created a new curd. When this new curd is drained, it becomes ricotta cheese.

Ingredients
2 gallons fresh whey (Note the word "fresh;" The whey should not be more than three hours old)
¼ cup cider vinegar
Salt (to taste)

Directions

1. Because this recipe calls for fresh whey, you are probably involved with other cheese making as you begin this procedure. The first step in this process calls for you to heat the whey to 200°. You can accomplish this by directly heating the whey on your stovetop (not in a double boiler) or by pouring the whey into a large slow cooker on high.

2. Gently stir vinegar into the whey.

3. Remove from heat.

4. At this point, small pieces of white coagulate curd will start to appear and float to the top of the liquid.

5. Line a colander with a large, doubled piece of cheesecloth. Make sure the cloth is large enough that you will be able to bring the corners together in a bag for the cheese to drain. Place the colander over a pot to catch the whey.

6. Gently pour the curds into the cheesecloth-lined colander.

7. Make a bag by tying the corners of the cheesecloth together.

8. Hang the bag of curds over the pot and allow to drain for about four hours, or until the whey stops dripping from the bag.

9. Remove the curds from the bag and place them in a bowl.

10. Salt to taste.

11. The curds can be kept in a sealed container in the refrigerator for a week.

Ricotta Salata

Ricotta salata is a drier, saltier ricotta than the standard ricotta; the "salata" in the name of this ricotta is salt. The difference in this recipe, though, is not only the salt, but also the fact that this ricotta is drier from pressing.

Traditionally, this cheese was made from ewe's milk. This recipe uses the fresh whey as the first ricotta recipe in this chapter does. You can also adapt this recipe to the whole-milk ricotta recipe that follows this one.

Ricotta salata is great as a pasta topper. You will especially enjoy it on top of pasta with pesto.

Ingredients
2 gallons fresh whey (Note the word "fresh;" the whey should not be more than three hours old)
¼ cup cider vinegar
1 tbsp cheese salt

Directions
1. Because this recipe calls for fresh whey, you are probably involved with other cheese making as you begin this procedure. The first step in this process calls for you to heat the whey to 200°, and you can accomplish this by directly heating the whey on your stovetop (not in a double boiler) or by pouring the whey into a large slow cooker on high.

2. Gently stir vinegar into the whey.

3. Remove from heat.

4. At this point, small pieces of white coagulate curd will start to appear and float to the top of the liquid.

5. Line a colander with a large, doubled piece of cheesecloth. Make sure the cloth is large enough that you will be able to bring the corners together in a bag for the cheese to drain. Place the colander over a pot to catch the whey.

6. Gently pour the curds into the cheesecloth-lined colander.

7. Make a bag by tying the corners of the cheesecloth together.

8. Hang the bag of curds over the pot and allow to drain for about four hours, or until the whey stops dripping from the bag.

9. Line a cheese mold with cheesecloth. Traditionally, molds for ricotta salata are wheel-shaped.

10. Place the cheese mold in a pan to catch the draining whey.

11. Transfer the curds from the colander into the cheese mold.

12. Fold the cheesecloth over the top to the cheese curd.

13. Place a saucer on top of the wrapped curd and place a 1-pound weight on the saucer.

14. Press with the 1-pound weight for an hour.

15. Remove the cheese from the mold and unwrap it.

16. Turn the cheese over and rewrap it.

17. Place the rewrapped cheese back into the mold and press with 1 pound for 12 hours.

18. Remove the cheese from the mold and unwrap it.

19. Lightly rub the surface of the cheese with salt and put it back in the mold. The cheesecloth is not necessary.

20. Place the cheese in a covered container.

21. Place the molded cheese in the refrigerator.

22. Flip the cheese in the mold every day for a week.

23. When you flip the cheese, lightly salt the surface.

24. If you notice mold beginning to develop in the surface of the cheese, you can remove it by gently rubbing it off with a piece of cheesecloth dampened with salt water.

25. Age the cheese in the refrigerator for two weeks to a month longer.

Whole-Milk Ricotta

There are many variations to the following recipe. One method will be offered here with suggestions to vary it as you experiment using whatever ingredients you may have on hand. *This recipe is the same as several of the quick cheese recipes offered in chapters 8 and 11 on yogurt and soft cheese.* The one ingredient that you must not alter in your experiments is whole milk. Note the name of the recipe; the recipes need the fat content of whole milk to be successful.

Ingredients
1 gallon whole milk
1 quart homemade cultured buttermilk
Salt (to taste)

Directions

1. Pour milk and buttermilk into a large, heavy-bottom, stainless-steel pot.

2. Slowly heat directly on stovetop to 180° to 185°.

3. Stir occasionally. You do not want the milk to scorch, but too much stirring will result in curds that are too small.

4. Remove pot from stove.

5. Allow milk to sit for 30 minutes. Do not stir during this time.

6. Line a colander with a large, doubled piece of cheesecloth. Make sure the cloth is large enough that you will be able to bring the corners together in a bag for the cheese to drain. Place the colander over a pot to catch the whey.

7. Gently pour the curds into the cheesecloth-lined colander.

8. Make a bag by tying the corners of the cheesecloth together.

9. Hang the bag of curds over the pot and allow to drain for 30 minutes to an hour, depending on what consistency you want your ricotta to be.

10. Remove the curds from the bag and place them in a bowl.

11. Salt to taste.

12. The ricotta can be kept in a sealed container in the refrigerator for a week.

Variations of this recipe involve using other ingredients rather than the cultured buttermilk. You can use 1 tsp of citric acid dissolved in ¼ cup of cool, unchlorinated water instead of the buttermilk.

You can also make this quick ricotta by using ⅓ cup white vinegar rather than the buttermilk. If you use the vinegar, do not add it until after you have heated the milk to 180° and removed the milk from the heat. Then, gently stir the vinegar and 1 tsp of salt into the milk. Allow the milk to sit for two hours before you continue the process in the manner described above.

You will notice in this whole-milk ricotta recipe that it is simply the process of adding an acid to the milk and heating. The acidic liquids of cultured buttermilk, vinegar, and the dissolved citric acid assist in the coagulation of the milk. In Chapter 2, you read about citric acid, vinegar, tartaric acid, or citrus juices such as lemon juice — that are used in various cheese recipes such as lemon cheese, mascarpone, and Mozzarella. If you are in the experimental mood and would like to try out other acids to make this quick ricotta, it is a simple enough recipe that you can play with it without worrying too much about what might go wrong.

Also note how similar this recipe is to the lemon cheese recipe offered in Chapter 5. If you made that recipe, you know how the use of ¼ cup of lemon juice worked not only to curdle the milk, but also to give the cheese a slight lemon flavor. Any highly acidic fruit can obtain the same results. Rather than using lemon juice, try ¼ cup of lime juice to make your ricotta. You can then use the resulting cheese to make a double-lime key lime pie. *See Chapter 16 for this outrageously wonderful treat.*

Mysost and Gjetost

Here are two cheese recipes in one. They are Norwegian in origin and are different only in the type of milk you use to make them. Mysost (pronounced my-sost) is made with the whey of cheese from cow's milk, and gjetost (pronounced yay-toast) comes from the whey of cheese made from goat's milk.

Though ricotta was a fairly simple whey cheese to make, mysost and gjetost are more difficult in that they take a long time. If you plan to make this cheese, get an early start and do not make any other plans for the day. The cheese is not aged, but you are required to cook it for six to 14 hours. Beyond the fact that it takes a long time to cook, you also need to use fresh whey. This means that you are also making another kind of cheese. Making mysost and gjetost is the mark of a true cheese making enthusiast.

Both can be made in a spreadable form or as a slicing cheese; the consistency is determined by the cooking time. The cheese is a traditional Scandinavian breakfast cheese and has a nutty, caramel-like flavor; it is great on toast. This cheese can also be shredded and combines very well with Mozzarella on pizza with sweet red onions and roasted red peppers.

Ingredients

Fresh cow's milk whey or goat's milk whey (Because of the cooking time required and the amount of reduction that occurs over the long cooking time, you want to start with whey from at least 2 gallons of milk)

Heavy cream (Cream is an optional ingredient. The amount that you use will determine the final texture and consistency of your cheese. For 2 gallons of milk, you can add up to 2 cups of heavy cream)

Note that you will want to have two large pots ready for this process. The whey will be cooked directly on the stovetop, so a double boiler is not necessary. However, you will need to process a large amount of whey one batch at a time in a blender or food processor. This means that you will be transferring the whey from one pot to another as the whey is processed.

Directions

1. Pour the fresh whey into a large, stainless-steel cooking pot.

2. Slowly heat the whey directly on the stovetop over medium heat until it comes to a boil. Watch the pot carefully, or the whey will boil over.

3. As the whey begins to boil, foam will appear on the surface.

4. Skim the foam off the surface of the whey with a slotted spoon.

5. Put the reserved foam in a bowl.

6. Allow the foam to cool for about 20 minutes before putting it in the refrigerator for use later on.

7. Lower the heat under the pot to a medium-low.

8. Cook the whey uncovered for six to 12 hours, stirring often.

9. Your goal is to reduce the volume of the whey by ¼ of the original amount.

10. This is a good time to prepare the molds you will need to pour the cheese into later on. Traditionally, this cheese is rectangular and about the size of a couple of sticks of butter. Place the molds in a shallow, heatproof pan. When you transfer the cheese to the molds, it will be very hot.

11. After you have reduced the volume, add the foam you removed earlier.

12. Cook for another 20 minutes.

13. The whey will thicken and resemble butterscotch pudding.

14. At this point, if you want a creamier cheese, add the cream by gently stirring it into the hot whey.

15. Remove the whey from the heat.

16. Very carefully transfer one batch at a time to a food processor or blender and process on a medium speed for 45 seconds to a minute. Take great care when doing this, as the whey is very hot. The amount of whey you process each time will be dictated by the size of your blender/food processor.

17. Pour the processed whey into another pot and continue to process each batch until you have processed all the whey.

18. Once you have processed all the whey, place the pot of processed whey on the stovetop over a low heat.

19. Stir constantly. If you do not constantly stir at this point, your cheese will develop a very grainy consistency.

20. The cheese will start to thicken considerably and come to the consistency of melted caramel.

21. Fill your kitchen sink with ice water.

22. When the cheese thickens to a hot caramel-like consistency, remove the pot from the stovetop and place it in the ice water-filled sink.

23. Keep stirring.

24. Stir while the pot is in the sink for two or three minutes to allow the cheese to cool slightly.

25. Pour the cheese into the molds.

26. Allow the cheese to set in the molds for ten hours.

27. Remove the cheese from the molds and wrap in wax paper.

This cheese will keep in your refrigerator for up to a month. If you do not wish to eat your cheese right away, it can be frozen in a sealed freezer bag and stored for as long as four months.

Troubleshooting — Whey Cheese

If your fresh whey ricotta fails to coagulate properly:

- You may have used whey that was not fresh. The most important part of any whey cheese recipe is to use fresh whey. If the whey is more than three hours old, the enzymes are no longer active, and this lack of activity will have a negative reaction on the texture and flavor of the cheese.

If your mysost develops a very grainy texture:

- You probably neglected to stir it consistently in the final reheating. Keep stirring it as you reheat the whey to thicken it and after you put the pot into the cold water bath, prior to placing it in the molds.

Other uses for your whey can be found in Chapter 16 of this book. If you find that you are overtaken by the amount of whey you are keeping, you may also consider using it to water your garden or pouring it onto a compost dump. Also, you can feed it to your pets; there is a good supply of vitamin B12 in whey that will make your pet's coat shine.

CASE STUDY: MARK MCAFEE

Organic Pastures Dairy Company
www.organicpastures.com

"We became involved in making cheese because consumers demanded truly raw cheese from organic pasture-fed cows, which is what we make. We have been doing it commercially as farmstead artisans for eight years. What we enjoy most about making cheese is the taste and nutritional value of the finished product. The hardest thing about making cheese is not having enough milk to fill all the orders we have.

"My favorite cheese to make is Truly Raw™ Cheddar cheese. Truly Raw Cheddar cheese is also my favorite cheese to eat. I love Swiss, as well.

My words of wisdom to those who are just getting started in making cheese are: It is all about your source of raw milk. Dead milk is not going to do it — it must be raw, organic, from grass-fed cows, and fresh."

CHAPTER 14

Hard Cheese

The primary difference between soft (or semi-soft) cheese and hard cheese is the amount of moisture that is in the end product. Hard cheese is hard because it is pressed more (to remove moisture) and aged for a longer period of time. The aging produces a drier cheese and one that, typically, is more flavorful.

Chapter 10 of this book covered the basic processes of cheese making. Some of the processes described there have not been used in the recipes for soft and semi-soft cheese, and this chapter will introduce you to a couple of new processes, such as coloring, bandaging, and waxing.

Once you have arrived at this point of your cheese-making experience, you are really beginning to understand how milk reacts to the agents that are introduced to it to coagulate and ripen it. You are becoming more knowledgeable on how to use your home equipment (especially your stove) to properly heat milk and curds. You have probably had several failures at this point, and you have likely learned what works and what does not work in creating a good curd, as well as how to handle a well-made curd.

Now you are ready to take the next step in this cheese-making process. While you are learning how to make hard cheese, you will produce feta, cheddar, Swiss, and several more popular varieties of hard cheese.

The best words of wisdom is advice you have received several times already, but it bears repeating: Be patient. Many of the cheeses you will be making from here on require a good amount of aging time; do not rush it. A good way to pass the time while you await the aging of your own wonderful cheese is to read and learn about other great cheeses of the world.

Steve Jenkins' book *Cheese Primer* is a great place to start to learn about the world of cheese. As you read *Cheese Primer*, visit the cheese section of your local grocer or specialty shop and treat yourself to some real cheddar. Better yet, find a local cheese maker and buy some locally made cheese. Visit that cheese maker and see if you can get a tour. Time will fly as you enjoy touring the world of cheese.

Feta

Start making hard cheese by making feta because it is relatively easy and employs all the cheese-making skills you have already learned.

Feta is a Greek word that came from the Italian word "fetta," meaning "slice," which refers to the way that the cheese is generally sold in Greece. The cheese is traditionally made in 30-pound wheels that are then sliced for sale in smaller amounts.

Traditionally, feta has been made with sheep's milk. However, today you will typically find goat's milk feta. The recipe below calls for goat's milk, but if you have a source for sheep's milk, you might want to experiment with that.

In the United States, feta is most often used in salads and sandwiches. It can be quite salty and goes well with a variety of greens and vegetables.

Ingredients

1 gallon whole goat's milk

¼ tsp lipase powder diluted in ¼ cup cool, unchlorinated water (This is optional for use if you desire a stronger-flavored cheese. If you use lipase powder, allow it to sit for 30 minutes after you dilute it)

$1/_8$ tsp calcium chloride dissolved in ¼ cup of cool, unchlorinated water (optional ingredient that will aid in the formation of the curd)

½ tsp powdered mesophilic starter (If you are using a prepared starter, use 4 ounces)

½ tablet vegetable rennet dissolved in ¼ cup of cool, unchlorinated water (Remember that if you are using powdered or rennet tablets, allow 20 to 30 minutes for the rennet to fully dissolve)

Salt (to taste)

Directions

1. Pour the milk into a stainless-steel bowl or pot.

2. Add diluted lipase if you choose to.

3. Place the bowl of milk into a hot water bath to bring the temperature of the milk to 85°.

4. Add calcium chloride if you choose to and stir well.

5. Add the mesophilic starter and stir well.

6. Add the diluted rennet mixture and stir gently.

7. Cover mixture and allow it to sit at 85° for an hour.

8. At this point, the curds will be a thick, yogurt-like consistency.

9. Cut the curds into 1-inch cubes.

10. Allow the curds to rest undisturbed for 15 minutes.

11. Gently stir the curds for 15 minutes at 85°.

12. Line a colander with a large, doubled piece of cheesecloth. Make sure the cloth is large enough that you will be able to bring the corners together in a bag for the cheese to drain. Place the colander over a pot to catch the whey.

13. Use a ladle to transfer the curds to the cheesecloth-lined colander.

14. If you have a hard time getting all of the curds with the ladle, you can gently pour the curds and whey into the colander.

15. Allow the curds to drain in the colander for ten minutes.

16. Bring the corners of the cheesecloth together and tie into a bag.

17. Hang the bag of curds over the pot and allow it to drain for six hours or until it reaches your desired consistency. You can do this at room temperature.

18. Untie the bag of cheese and turn the cheese out onto a large cutting board.

19. Cut the curds into 1-inch cubes.

20. Salt the cubes to taste.

21. Transfer the cheese to a bowl and cover the bowl.

22. Place the covered bowl of cheese in the refrigerator for five days.

23. This feta will keep in an airtight container in your refrigerator for up to two weeks.

An optional way of making the feta recipe shown above is to use ¼ cup buttermilk as your starter rather than the ½ tsp powdered mesophilic starter. You would follow the recipe as described.

Muenster

Muenster is the next logical step to take after feta in learning to make hard cheese because it is a relatively easy cheese to make in that it has few ingredients and employs processes that you have learned already. It takes some pressing and aging, but your patience will pay off with a great cheese that is versatile and quite tasty.

Muenster is a wonderful cheese to use for recipes that call for a good melting cheese. You can use Muenster for grilled cheese sandwiches, macaroni and cheese, grated over salads, or all by itself to complement fresh fruit.

Ingredients

1 gallon whole milk (You can use cow's milk or goat's milk for this recipe)

½ tablet vegetable rennet dissolved in ¼ cup of cool, unchlorinated water (Remember that if you are using powdered or rennet tablets, allow 20 to 30 minutes for the rennet to fully dissolve)

Salt (to taste)

Directions

1. Pour the milk into a stainless-steel bowl or pot.

2. Place the bowl of milk into a hot water bath to bring the temperature of the milk to 85°. Alternatively, you can heat the milk in a double boiler.

3. Remove the pot of milk from the heat and allow it to sit for five minutes.

4. Add the diluted rennet mixture and stir gently.

5. Cover mixture and allow it to sit undisturbed for an hour.

6. At this point, the curds will be a thick, yogurt-like consistency.

7. Cut the curds into 1-inch cubes.

8. You can add a little salt at this point by sprinkling 1 to 2 tsp over the curds.

9. Allow the curds to rest undisturbed for 15 minutes.

10. Return the pot of curds to the warm water in a double boiler and very gently turn the curds. Your goal here is to gently bring the curds from the bottom of the pot to the top. Again, the emphasis is on "gentle." If you stir the curds too vigorously, it will have a negative effect on the consistency of your cheese. The gentle turning of the curds helps heat them evenly and distribute the added salt.

11. Allow the curds to rest undisturbed for 15 minutes.

12. Line a colander with a large, doubled piece of cheesecloth. Make sure the cloth is large enough that you will be able to bring the corners together in a bag for the cheese to drain. Place the colander over a pot to catch the whey.

13. Use a ladle to transfer the curds to the cheesecloth-lined colander.

14. Allow the curds to drain for 30 minutes.

15. Line a cheese mold with cheesecloth. Ideally, you will want to use a 1-pound mold (a mold large enough to accommodate 1 pound of cheese).

16. You will be pressing this cheese with 40 pounds of weight, so use a mold from a cheese press, one that is made of sturdy, food-grade plastic or stainless steel.

17. Place the cheese mold in a pan to catch the draining whey.

18. When the curd has reached room temperature, transfer the curds from the colander into the cheese mold. You should pack the curds rather tightly into the mold.

19. Fold the cheesecloth over the top to the cheese curd.

20. Place a follower on top of the wrapped curd and press the curd with 40 pounds of pressure for 12 hours.

21. Remove the cheese from the mold and unwrap it.

22. Turn the cheese over and rewrap it.

23. Place the rewrapped cheese back into the mold and press with 40 pounds for 12 hours.

24. Lightly rub the exterior of the cheese with salt.

25. Place the cheese on a cheese mat and place a saucer on top of the cheese to prevent the top of the cheese from becoming too dry.

26. Flip the cheese once a day for five or six days, lightly salting the exterior of the cheese each time you flip it.

27. The cheese will develop a soft rind after a couple of days.

28. The cheese is ready after it has developed the rind.

29. The longer you allow your cheese to sit, the more intense the flavor will be.

30. You can let your cheese develop for as long as a month.

31. Muenster cheese may be frozen for up to three months.

32. Once you slice into your Muenster cheese, you should use it within a week's time.

Cheddar Cheese

After Mozzarella, cheddar is the most popular natural cheese in the United States. There are so many recipes for making cheddar and so much to say about it that an entire book could be devoted entirely to this popular cheese. Offered here is a little history and two very good recipes for making your own home-made cheddar cheese.

When you think of cheddar cheese, it is probable that you first think of what is known in cheese circles as "American cheddar." This is not necessarily American cheese, but cheddar cheese produced in factories for mass consumption by American consumers. This is a cheese than can boast the word "natural," but because of the way in which it is produced, it lacks the complexity of flavor of its cousin farmhouse cheddar.

Historically, it is thought that the cheese is named after the town of Cheddar, England, which is where the original Cheddar Caves are. These caves have been used as a place for aging cheese. However, "cheddaring" is also a milling process that is specific to this type of cheese, as the curds of cheddar cheese are cooked twice. The first cooking of the curds occurs in much the same manner as a standard cheese recipe; after that, the curds are then cut and cooked a second time.

There are recipes for cheddar cheese that do not include this cheddaring process. One of those recipes is included here as a good place to start to learn to make cheddar cheese.

Chances are, when you think of cheddar cheese, the cheese you see in your mind's eye is orange. The orange color does not come from a natural part of the cheese-making process, but is color that is added to the cheese. Most recipes that produce an orange-colored cheese call for the ingredient liquid annatto cheese coloring. This is a natural extract from the seeds of a South American shrub called achiote. Uncolored cheddar cheese ranges from a straw-like color to white, and the color is determined by the diet of the cow(s) that gave the milk. Cheddar is traditionally colored to do away with the seasonal color variations that are a result of the cow's diet.

Both of the recipes offered here can be considered "farmhouse" cheddar recipes. The farmhouse label comes from the fact that these are cheeses that have traditionally been made in people's houses. The first recipe is what is known as a "stirred curd" recipe, and the second involves the milling process of cheddaring.

Ingredients

2 gallons whole milk (cow's milk or goat's milk)

½ tsp powdered mesophilic starter (If you are using a prepared starter, use 4 ounces)

2 drops of liquid annatto cheese coloring diluted in ¼ cup of unchlorinated water (optional ingredient that can be found in cheese supply stores or online retailers)

½ tablet vegetable rennet dissolved in ¼ cup of cool, unchlorinated water (Remember that if you are using powdered or rennet tablets, allow 20 to 30 minutes for the rennet to fully dissolve)

2 tbsp cheese salt

Cheese wax

Directions

1. Pour the milk into a stainless-steel pot of a double boiler.

2. Bring the temperature of the milk to 90°.

3. Add the mesophilic starter and stir well.

4. Cover the mixture and allow 45 minutes to ripen at 90°.

5. If you are using the liquid annatto cheese coloring, add it now. Stir the mixture well to evenly distribute the coloring.

6. Add the diluted rennet mixture and stir gently for one minute.

7. Cover mixture and allow it to sit at 90° for 45 minutes to an hour.

8. At this point, the curds will be a thick, yogurt-like consistency.

9. Use a clean finger or a curd knife to check that the curds break cleanly when you cut then or insert your finger.

10. Cut the curds into ¼-inch cubes.

11. Allow the curds to sit for 20 minutes.

12. Slowly heat curds to 100°. Do this by increasing the temperature of the curds by 2° every five minutes. It should take you about 30 minutes to bring the curds to 100°.

13. Very gently stir as you heat the curds, allowing the curds to be evenly heated as it prevents them from sticking together.

14. When the temperature of the curds reaches 100°, hold that temperature for 30 minutes. Continue to gently stir the curds during this 30-minute time period.

15. After 30 minutes, turn the heat off and allow the curds to set for five minutes.

16. Line a colander with a large, doubled piece of cheesecloth. Place the colander over a pot to catch the whey.

17. Drain the curds by pouring them into the cheesecloth-lined colander.

18. Allow the curds to drain for about 15 minutes. If you allow the curds to drain too long, they will start to stick together.

19. As soon as the curds have stopped dripping whey, put them back into the pot you cooked them in.

20. Place the pot of curds back into the 100° water of the double boiler.

21. Use your clean hands to gently stir the curds and break up any pieces that have stuck together.

22. Add cheese salt and gently mix with your hands.

23. Let the curds sit at 100° for an hour, stirring every five minutes.

24. Line a cheese mold with cheesecloth. Ideally, you will want to use a 2-pound mold (a mold large enough to accommodate 2 pounds of cheese).

25. Transfer the curds to the cheesecloth-lined cheese mold.

26. You should pack the curds rather tightly into the mold.

27. Fold the cheesecloth over the top of the curd.

28. You will be pressing this cheese with up to 50 pounds of weight, so use a mold from a cheese press, one that is made of sturdy, food-grade plastic or stainless steel.

29. Place the cheese mold in a pan to catch the draining whey.

30. Place a follower on top of the wrapped curd and press the curd with 15 pounds of pressure for ten minutes.

31. Remove the cheese from the mold and unwrap it.

32. Turn the cheese over and rewrap it.

33. Place the rewrapped cheese back into the mold and press with 30 pounds for ten minutes.

34. Remove the cheese from the mold and unwrap it.

35. Turn the cheese over and rewrap it.

36. Place the rewrapped cheese back into the mold and press with 40 pounds for two hours.

37. Remove the cheese from the mold and unwrap it.

38. Turn the cheese over and rewrap it.

39. Place the rewrapped cheese back into the mold and press with 50 pounds for 24 hours.

40. Remove the cheese from the mold and unwrap it.

41. Place the cheese on a cheese mat and allow it to sit at room temperature until it is dry to the touch.

42. Flip the cheese daily to help it dry evenly. This will take up to five days.

43. Wax the cheese. *See notes on waxing cheese in Chapter 10.*

44. Allow the cheese to age at 45° to 55° for two to six months.

Cheddared Cheddar Cheese

This recipe is considered to be a traditional one in that it includes the cheddaring technique that gave the cheese its name.

Ingredients

2 gallons whole milk (cow's milk or goat's milk)

½ tsp powdered mesophilic starter (if you are using a prepared starter, use 4 ounces)

2 drops of liquid annatto cheese coloring diluted in ¼ cup of unchlorinated water (optional)

½ tablet vegetable rennet dissolved in ¼ cup of cool, unchlorinated water (Remember that if you are using powdered or rennet tablets, allow 20 to 30 minutes for the rennet to fully dissolve)

2 tbsp cheese salt

Cheese wax

Directions

1. Pour the milk into a stainless-steel pot of a double boiler.

2. Bring the temperature of the milk to 85°.

3. Add the mesophilic starter and stir well.

4. Cover the mixture and allow one hour for mixture to ripen at 85°.

5. If you are using the liquid annatto cheese coloring, add it now. Stir the mixture well to evenly distribute the coloring.

6. Add the diluted rennet mixture and stir gently for one minute.

7. Cover mixture and allow it to sit at 85° for 45 minutes to an hour.

8. At this point, the curds will be a thick, yogurt-like consistency.

9. Use a clean finger or a curd knife to check that the curds break cleanly when you cut them or insert your finger.

10. Cut the curds into ¼-inch cubes.

11. Allow the curds to sit for 20 minutes.

12. Slowly heat curds to 100°. Do this by increasing the temperature of the curds by 2° every five minutes. It should take you about 30 to 45 minutes to bring the curds to 100°.

13. Very gently stir as you heat the curds, allowing the curds to be evenly heated to prevent them from sticking together.

14. When the temperature of the curds reaches 100°, hold that temperature for 30 minutes. Continue to gently stir the curds during this 30-minute time period.

15. After 30 minutes, turn the heat off and allow the curds to set for five minutes.

16. Line a colander with a large, doubled piece of cheesecloth. Place the colander over a pot to catch the whey.

17. Drain the curds by pouring them into the cheesecloth-lined colander.

18. Allow the curds to drain for about 15 to 20 minutes. The curds will become a single mass of curd, which is what you are aiming for. Note the difference between the curds at this point in the recipe as opposed to the curds in the previous recipe in which you were aiming to have them not stick together.

19. Transfer the drained curds to a sterilized cutting board.

20. At this point, the curds should be a singular mass. This mass should be sliced in ½-inch slices in the same manner that you slice a loaf of bread.

21. Transfer the sliced curd back to the pot of double boiler. The pot of curds will be surrounded by 100° water.

22. Allow the curds to ripen at 100° for two hours.

23. During the two-hour ripening period, turn the curds over every 30 minutes.

24. After two hours, the curds will be somewhat rubbery to the touch.

25. Remove the pot of curds from the double boiler.

26. Use a curd knife to cut the curds into ¾-inch cubes.

27. Return the pot of curds to the double boiler.

28. Allow the pot of curds to sit surrounded by the warm water of the double boiler for about 45 minutes.

29. Gently turn the curds every five to ten minutes to expel a little more whey. Do not stir vigorously.

30. Remove the pot of curds from the double boiler.

31. Add the salt and gently stir.

32. Line a cheese mold with cheesecloth. Ideally, you will want to use a 2-pound mold (a mold large enough to accommodate 2 pounds of cheese).

33. Transfer the curds to the cheesecloth-lined cheese mold.

34. You should pack the curds rather tightly into the mold.

35. Fold the cheesecloth over the top of the curd.

36. You will be pressing this cheese with up to 40 pounds of weight, so use a mold from a cheese press, made of sturdy, food-grade plastic or stainless steel.

37. Place the cheese mold in a pan to catch the draining whey.

38. Place a follower on top of the wrapped curd and press the curd with 40 pounds of pressure for 12 hours.

39. Remove the cheese from the mold and unwrap it.

40. Turn the cheese over and rewrap it.

41. Place the rewrapped cheese back into the mold and press with 40 pounds for 12 hours.

42. Remove the cheese from the mold and unwrap it.

43. Turn the cheese over and rewrap it.

44. Place the rewrapped cheese back into the mold and press with 40 pounds for 12 hours.

45. Remove the cheese from the mold and unwrap it.

46. Place the cheese on a cheese mat and allow it to sit at room temperature until it is dry to the touch.

47. Flip the cheese daily to help it dry evenly. This will take up to five days.

48. Wax the cheese. *See notes on waxing cheese in Chapter 10.*

49. Allow the cheese to age at 45° to 55° for two to 12 months.

Additions to Cheddar Cheese

If you have shopped for cheddar cheese, you know that there are not only a variety of cheddar cheese types (farmhouse, white, and stirred curd to name a few), but you also know that you can get cheddar that has been flavored with various herbs and seasonings, such as caraway, chives, sage, and pepper. There are numerous ways to go about adding these flavors. Here are basic directions for spicing up your cheddar.

1. Simmer about ½ cup of unchlorinated water in a small saucepan.

2. Add 2 to 4 tbsp of your chosen herb or spice. You can choose to use fresh or dried ingredients. Experiment with quantities; start on the lower end of the scale and increase or decrease to taste. Often, the taste will not be

determined by quantity as much as it will be by quality and freshness of ingredients.

3. Boil the herbs/spices/seasonings in the water for ten to 15 minutes.

4. Strain the water into a small bowl and allow it to cool.

5. Save the boiled herbs/spices/seasonings.

6. Add the strained water to the milk when you initially heat the milk in the first step of your cheese making.

7. Add the reserved herbs/spices/seasonings when you add salt during the cheese making.

8. Continue the cheese-making process as directed.

Jack

Monterey Jack is a type of cheese that is part of a larger family of cheeses known as Jack cheese. There are a number of myths as to how this cheese got its name. One such story refers to the kind of press that was first employed to create the cheese, which was called a housejack. This derivation claims that the cheese is of Spanish origin and was brought to California by Franciscan monks. Another claim is that a fellow named David Jacks developed the cheese in Monterey, California, in the late 1800s.

The family of Jack cheeses are all fairly similar and vary only due to aging, additions to the cheese, and type of milk used to make the cheese. The varieties of Jack cheese include Monterey Jack, Dry Jack, and Pepper Jack.

The recipe offered below is for a straight Jack cheese. If you use milk from the Monterey area of California, you might claim that it is Monterey Jack. If you would like a Pepper Jack, you can follow the directions offered above for adding ingredients to cheddar cheese. You may add chopped jalapenos to Jack cheese using the same method.

Ingredients

2 gallons whole milk (cow's milk or goat's milk)

½ tsp powdered mesophilic starter (If you are using a prepared starter, use 4 ounces)

¹/₈ tsp calcium chloride dissolved in ¼ cup cool, unchlorinated water (Allow the calcium chloride to dissolve for 20 minutes prior to using it. Adding calcium chloride is optional for this recipe, but you will find that it helps the curd structure)

½ tablet vegetable rennet dissolved in ¼ cup of cool, unchlorinated water (Remember that if you are using powdered or rennet tablets, allow 20 to 30 minutes for the rennet to fully dissolve)

1 tbsp cheese salt

Cheese wax

Directions

1. Pour the milk into a stainless-steel pot of a double boiler.

2. Bring the temperature of the milk to 88°.

3. Add the mesophilic starter and stir well.

4. Cover the mixture and allow 30 minutes to ripen at 88°.

5. If you are using the calcium chloride, add it now. Stir the mixture well to evenly distribute.

6. Add the diluted rennet mixture and stir gently for one minute.

7. Cover mixture and allow it to sit at 90° for 45 minutes to an hour.

8. At this point, the curds will be a thick, yogurt-like consistency.

9. Use a clean finger or a curd knife to check that the curds break cleanly when you cut them or insert your finger.

10. Cut the curds into ¼-inch cubes.

11. Hold the temperature for 40 minutes while occasionally stirring the curds.

12. Slowly heat curds to 100°. Do this by increasing the temperature of the curds by 2° every five minutes. It should take you about 30 minutes to bring the curds to 100°.

13. Very gently stir as you heat the curds, allowing the curds to be evenly heated to prevent them from sticking together.

14. When the temperature of the curds reaches 100°, hold that temperature for 30 minutes. Continue to gently stir the curds during this 30-minute time period.

15. After 30 minutes, turn the heat off and allow the curds to sit for five minutes.

16. Very carefully pour off the whey from the curds.

17. Allow the curds to sit for 30 minutes, stirring gently frequently to keep them from sticking together. The target temperature of 100° should be maintained at this time.

18. Line a colander with a large, doubled piece of cheesecloth. Place the colander over a pot to catch the whey.

19. Drain the curds by ladling them into the cheesecloth-lined colander.

20. Allow the curds to drain for about five minutes. If you allow the curds to drain too long, they will start to stick together.

21. Add cheese salt and gently mix.

22. Line a cheese mold with cheesecloth. Ideally, you will want to use a 2-pound mold (a mold large enough to accommodate 2 pounds of cheese).

23. Transfer the curds to the cheesecloth-lined cheese mold.

24. You should pack the curds rather tightly into the mold.

25. Fold the cheesecloth over the top of the curd.

26. You will be pressing this cheese with up to 40 pounds of weight, so use a mold from a cheese press, one that is made of sturdy, food-grade plastic or stainless steel.

27. Place the cheese mold in a pan to catch the draining whey.

28. Place a follower on top of the wrapped curd and press the curd with 10 pounds of pressure for 15 minutes.

29. Remove the cheese from the mold and unwrap it.

30. Turn the cheese over and rewrap it.

31. Place the rewrapped cheese back into the mold and press with 30 pounds for 30 minutes.

32. Remove the cheese from the mold and unwrap it.

33. Turn the cheese over and rewrap it.

34. Place the rewrapped cheese back into the mold and press with 40 pounds for 12 hours.

35. Remove the cheese from the mold and unwrap it.

36. Place the cheese on a cheese mat and allow it to sit at room temperature until it is dry to the touch.

37. Flip the cheese daily to help it dry evenly. This will take up to five days.

38. Wax the cheese. *See notes on waxing cheese in Chapter 10.*

39. Allow the cheese to age at 45° to 55° for one to three months.

Colby

Colby cheese is a relative newcomer to the world of cheese. Colby was created in Colby, Wisconsin, near the turn of the 20th century. It is very much like cheddar cheese, but to make it you need to learn a cheese-making process that will be new to you. Colby is what is known as a "washed curd" cheese. Another washed curd cheese that you will learn to make is Gouda (a recipe for Gouda follows this Colby recipe). Washing the curd is exactly what it sounds like: You replace the whey that separated from the curd in the cooking process with hot water.

Colby is a mild cheese that is great for grilled cheese sandwiches, macaroni and cheese, and a plate of nachos. Colby is an all-purpose cheese and is, in many ways, a true American cheese, as it was first developed in America.

Ingredients

2 gallons whole milk (cow's milk or goat's milk)

½ tsp powdered mesophilic starter (If you are using a prepared starter, use 4 ounces)

2 drops of liquid annatto cheese coloring diluted in ¼ cup of unchlorinated water (optional)

½ tablet vegetable rennet dissolved in ¼ cup of cool, unchlorinated water (Remember that if you are using powdered or rennet tablets, allow 20 to 30 minutes for the rennet to fully dissolve)

2 tbsp cheese salt

Cheese wax

Directions

1. Pour the milk into a stainless-steel pot of a double boiler.

2. Bring the temperature of the milk to 85°.

3. Add the mesophilic starter and stir well.

4. Cover the mixture and allow one hour to ripen at 85°.

5. If you are using the liquid annatto cheese coloring, add it now. Stir the mixture well to evenly distribute the coloring.

6. Add the diluted rennet mixture and stir gently for one minute.

7. Cover mixture and allow it to sit at 85° for 45 minutes to an hour.

8. At this point, the curds will be a thick, yogurt-like consistency.

9. Use a clean finger or a curd knife to check that the curds break cleanly when you cut them or insert your finger.

10. Cut the curds into ½-inch cubes.

11. Allow the curds to sit for 15 minutes.

12. Slowly heat curds to 100°. Do this by increasing the temperature of the curds by 2° every five minutes. It should take you about 30 to 45 minutes to bring the curds to 100°.

13. Very gently stir as you heat the curds, allowing the curds to be evenly heated to prevent them from sticking together.

14. When the temperature of the curds reaches 100°, hold that temperature for 30 minutes. Continue to gently stir the curds during this 30-minute time period.

15. Remove the pot of curds from the double boiler and allow it to sit undisturbed for five minutes.

16. The curds should be at the bottom of the pot, covered by the liquid whey.

17. Fill a separate bowl or pot with 60° water. You will need the same amount of water as whey that you will remove from the pot of curds.

18. Use a measuring cup to remove the whey that covers the curds. Keep track of the amount of whey you remove from the pot.

19. As the curds sit at the bottom of the pot, there is a reserve of whey in the pot above the curds. Remove all the whey that sits above the level of the curds. Keep track of the amount of whey that you remove from the pot.

20. Add the same amount of 60° water as whey removed to the curds. Or, add 60° water until the temperature of the curds reaches 80°.

21. Gently stir the curds as you add the water.

22. After the curds reach 80°, maintain that temperature for 20 minutes.

23. Stir the curds frequently over the 20-minute hold period.

24. Line a colander with a large, doubled piece of cheesecloth.

25. Drain the curds by pouring them into the cheesecloth-lined colander.

26. Allow the curds to drain for about 20 minutes. If you allow the curds to drain too long, they will start to stick together.

27. As soon as the curds have stopped dripping, put them back into the pot you cooked them in.

28. Use your clean hands to gently stir the curds and break up (mill) any pieces that have stuck together.

29. Mill the cheese curd into pieces that are about ¼-inch big.

30. Add cheese salt and gently mix with your hands.

31. Line a cheese mold with cheesecloth. Ideally, you will want to use a 2-pound mold (a mold large enough to accommodate 2 pounds of cheese).

32. Transfer the curds to the cheesecloth-lined cheese mold.

33. Pack the curds rather tightly into the mold.

34. Fold the cheesecloth over the top of the curd.

35. You will be pressing this cheese with up to 50 pounds of weight, so use a mold from a cheese press made of sturdy, food-grade plastic or stainless steel.

36. Place the cheese mold in a pan to catch the draining whey.

37. Place a follower on top of the wrapped curd and press the curd with 20 pounds of pressure for 30 minutes.

38. Remove the cheese from the mold and unwrap it.

39. Turn the cheese over and rewrap it.

40. Place the rewrapped cheese back into the mold and press with 20 pounds of pressure for 30 minutes.

41. Remove the cheese from the mold and unwrap it.

42. Turn the cheese over and rewrap it.

43. Place the rewrapped cheese back into the mold and press with 40 pounds for one hour.

44. Remove the cheese from the mold and unwrap it.

45. Turn the cheese over and rewrap it.

46. Place the rewrapped cheese back into the mold and press with 50 pounds for 12 hours.

47. Remove the cheese from the mold and unwrap it.

48. Place the cheese on a cheese mat and allow it to sit at room temperature until it is dry to the touch.

49. Flip the cheese four to six times a day to help it dry evenly. This will take up to five days.

50. Wax the cheese. *See notes on waxing cheese in Chapter 10.*

51. Allow the cheese to age at 45° to 55° for two to three months.

Gouda

Gouda (pronounced "how-da") is another washed-curd cheese. It originated in the Danish town of Gouda and is a smooth-textured cheese with a sharp flavor.

Ingredients

2 gallons whole milk (cow's milk or goat's milk)

½ tsp powdered mesophilic starter (If you are using a prepared starter, use 4 ounces)

½ tablet vegetable rennet dissolved in ¼ cup of cool, unchlorinated water (Remember, if you are using powdered or rennet tablets, allow 20 to 30 minutes for the rennet to fully dissolve)

2 quarts unchlorinated water heated to 175°

2 pounds of cheese salt for brine solution

1 gallon cold water

Cheese wax

Directions

1. Pour the milk into a stainless-steel pot of a double boiler.

2. Bring the temperature of the milk to 90°.

3. Add the mesophilic starter and stir well.

4. Cover the mixture and allow 15 minutes to ripen at 90°.

5. Add the diluted rennet mixture and stir gently for one minute.

6. Cover mixture and allow it to sit at 90° for two hours.

7. At this point, the curds will be a thick, yogurt-like consistency.

8. Use a clean finger or a curd knife to check that the curds break cleanly when you cut them or insert your finger.

9. If the curds do not produce a clean break, allow them to sit for another 30 minutes.

10. Cut the curds into ½-inch cubes.

11. Allow the curds to sit for five minutes at 90°.

12. The curds should be at the bottom of the pot, covered by the liquid whey.

13. Use a measuring cup to remove the whey that covers the curds.

14. Slowly add some of the 175° water until the temperature of the curds reaches 92°. It should take about 2 cups of the hot water to accomplish this.

15. Continue to gently stir as you add the hot water.

16. After the curds reach 92°, allow them to sit for ten minutes, giving them an occasional gentle stir.

17. Use a measuring cup to remove the whey that covers the curds.

18. Slowly add some of the 175° water until the temperature of the curds reaches 92°. It should take about 2 cups of the hot water to accomplish this.

19. Continue to gently stir as you add the hot water.

20. After the curds reach 92°, allow them to sit for ten minutes, giving them an occasional gentle stir.

21. Use a measuring cup to remove the whey that covers the curds.

22. Slowly add some of the 175° water until the temperature of the curds reaches 100°. It should take about 3 cups of the hot water to accomplish this.

23. Continue to gently stir as you add the hot water.

24. After the curds reach 100°, allow them to sit for 30 minutes at this temperature, giving them an occasional gentle stir.

25. Line a colander with a large, doubled piece of cheesecloth.

26. Drain the curds by pouring them into the cheesecloth-lined colander.

27. Allow the curds to drain for just a couple of minutes.

28. Transfer the warm curds to a 2-pound cheese mold lined with cheese-cloth.

29. Be gentle with the curds as you transfer them, trying not to break them up.

30. Fold the cheesecloth over the top of the curds.

31. You will be pressing this cheese with up to 50 pounds of weight, so use a mold from a cheese press made of sturdy, food-grade plastic or stainless steel.

32. Place the cheese mold in a pan to catch the draining whey.

33. Place a follower on top of the wrapped curd and press the curd with 20 pounds of pressure for 20 minutes.

34. Remove the cheese from the mold and unwrap it.

35. Turn the cheese over and rewrap it.

36. Place the rewrapped cheese back into the mold and press with 40 pounds of pressure for 20 minutes.

37. Remove the cheese from the mold and unwrap it.

38. Turn the cheese over and rewrap it.

39. Place the rewrapped cheese back into the mold and press with 40 pounds for 30 minutes.

40. Remove the cheese from the mold and unwrap it.

41. Turn the cheese over and rewrap it.

42. Place the rewrapped cheese back into the mold and press with 50 pounds for 12 hours.

43. Remove the cheese from the mold and unwrap it.

44. Prepare a saturated brine solution with 2 pounds of cheese salt and 1 gallon of cold water.

45. Soak the cheese in the brine solution for six hours. Flip the cheese twice during this period.

46. Remove the cheese from the brine solution and pat dry with a paper towel.

47. Place the cheese on a drying mat and allow to dry at 50° for three weeks.

48. Flip the cheese daily as it dries.

49. Wax the cheese. *See notes on waxing cheese in Chapter 10.*

50. Allow the cheese to age at 45° to 55° for three to six months.

51. Aging the cheese longer will allow it to develop a more pronounced flavor. You can age this cheese for as long as nine months.

Swiss Cheese

This is another cheese type that entire books can be written about. When you think of Swiss cheese, you probably think about the white cheese with holes that you find in the grocer's dairy case or at the deli, but there is so much more to Swiss cheese. You buy it as a brick, sliced, or thinly deli-sliced for sandwiches. Like cheddar, the name "Swiss" is generic and describes not a kind of cheese, but more of a type of cheese. There are many varieties of cheese that are Swiss.

Even if you recognize Swiss cheese by its color and holes, you still have to sort out the variety of Swiss cheeses that are white with holes. You might have a "traditional" Swiss, a Baby Swiss, or an Emmenthal. The differences in the various kinds of Swiss cheese, like the differences in cheddars, come from the variety of ways that the basic cheese is produced.

Emmenthal

The most traditional of the Swiss cheeses is Emmenthal, which is named for the valley in Switzerland where the cheese originated. Like all Swiss cheeses, Emmenthal has a somewhat nutty flavor and, of course, holes.

Ingredients

2 gallons whole milk (cow's milk or goat's milk)

½ tsp powdered thermophilic starter (If you are using a prepared starter, use 4 ounces)

1 tsp *Propionic shermanii* powder dissolved in ¼ cup of warm milk (These are a bacteria that make carbon dioxide as they react with milk. The carbon dioxide production is what makes the distinctive holes in Swiss cheese)

½ tablet vegetable rennet dissolved in ¼ cup of cool, unchlorinated water (Remember that if you are using powdered or rennet tablets, allow 20 to 30 minutes for the rennet to fully dissolve)

2 pounds of cheese salt for brine solution

1 gallon cold water

Directions

1. Pour the milk into a stainless-steel pot of a double boiler.

2. Bring the temperature of the milk to 90°.

3. Add the thermophilic starter and stir well.

4. Remove ¼ cup of the warm milk from the pot and place it in a small cup or bowl.

5. Add the *Propionic shermanii* to the ¼ cup of warm milk that was removed from the pot. Mix the *Propionic shermanii* to make sure that it is dissolved.

6. Pour the *Propionic shermanii* mixture back into the pot with the 90° milk.

7. Cover the mixture and allow 15 minutes to ripen at 90°.

8. Add the diluted rennet mixture and stir gently for one minute.

9. Cover mixture and allow it to sit at 90° for 30 minutes.

10. At this point, the curds will be a thick, yogurt-like consistency.

11. Use a clean finger or a curd knife to check that the curds break cleanly when you cut them or insert your finger.

12. If the curds do not produce a clean break, allow them to sit for another 15 minutes.

13. Cut the curds into ¼-inch cubes.

14. Holding the curds at a temperature of 90° for 45 to 60 minutes, gently stir them with a whisk. Your goal, as you stir the curds, is to get the curds into a fairly uniform shape and to ensure that no whey is on the surface or sides of the pot. This method of working the curds is called foreworking.

15. Slowly increase the temperature of the curds to 120°. You should take about 30 to 45 minutes to do this.

16. As you increase the curd temperature, stir frequently with a whisk.

17. When you reach the targeted 120°, hold that temperature for 30 minutes.

18. Continue to stir the curds with a whisk.

19. At this point, your curds will be quite small.

20. You can test to see if your curds are ready to proceed by removing 1 tbsp of curds from the pot and rubbing them together with your fingers in the palm of your hand. If they curds easily break apart, they are ready. If the curds do not easily break, cook them for another 15 to 20 minutes and test them again.

21. When the curds are ready and you move on to the next step, it is important to know that you need to keep things moving at this point. The curds need to be molded and pressed while they are still hot.

22. Prepare a 2-pound cheese mold by lining it with cheesecloth. Place the cheese mold in a pan to catch the draining whey.

23. Use a slotted ladle to transfer the warm curds to a 2-pound cheese mold lined with cheesecloth.

24. Fold the cheesecloth over the top of the curd.

25. Place a follower on top of the wrapped curd and press the curd with 10 pounds of pressure for 15 minutes. The pressing should be done at room temperature.

26. Remove the cheese from the mold and unwrap it.

27. Turn the cheese over and rewrap it.

28. Place the rewrapped cheese back into the mold and press with 15 pounds of pressure for 30 minutes.

29. Remove the cheese from the mold and unwrap it.

30. Turn the cheese over and rewrap it.

31. Place the rewrapped cheese back into the mold and press with 15 pounds for two hours.

32. Remove the cheese from the mold and unwrap it.

33. Turn the cheese over and rewrap it.

34. Place the rewrapped cheese back into the mold and press with 15 pounds for 12 hours.

35. Remove the cheese from the mold and unwrap it.

36. Prepare a saturated brine solution with 2 pounds of cheese salt and 1 gallon of cold water.

37. Soak the cheese in the brine solution for 12 hours. Flip the cheese three or four times over this period.

38. Remove the cheese from the brine solution and pat dry with a paper towel.

39. Place the cheese on a cheese board and allow it to dry at 55° with 85 percent humidity for one week.

40. During this week, flip the cheese over every day and wipe it with a clean cloth dampened with brine solution.

41. Remove the cheese from the cooler and allow it to sit at room temperature for three weeks.

42. During this period, again, flip the cheese over every day and wipe it with a clean cloth dampened with brine solution.

43. After three weeks, the cheese should be aged at a temperature of 45° and 85 percent humidity for three months.

44. As the cheese ages, you should flip it over and wipe off any surface mold with a brine-dampened cloth several times a week.

Compared to other cheese making, Swiss cheese is a difficult cheese to create. The process is lengthy, and you employ various techniques in heating, handling, and shaping the curd. You press and age the cheese over an extended period of time, and the cheese needs to be managed and watched carefully throughout the entire production process.

If you are comfortable and confident in your ability to make Swiss cheese, you are probably prepared to move on to the final step in learning to make cheese, which is making bacteria- and mold-ripened cheese. Before you move on to making these cheeses, go back over your notes and familiarize yourself with the successes and failures you have experienced. Your notes will serve you well as you move on to the most challenging cheese-making recipes.

Troubleshooting Hard Cheeses

If your cheese is very dry:

- You may have cooked your curd at too high a temperature. Next time, watch the temperature more closely as you cook and keep it at the level recommended by the recipe.

- You may have over-stirred the curds. Next time, treat the curds gentler.

- You may not have added enough rennet. Try adding a little more rennet the next time you make the recipe.

If your cheese develops an excessive amount of surface mold as you are air drying it:

- You may be drying the cheese in a place that is excessively humid. Move the cheese to a less humid place or lower the humidity in the area the cheese is being dried.

- The board or mat you are drying your cheese on may not be clean. Be sure to start with a clean surface. Remove the cheese from the drying board or mat and wipe the cheese with a brine or vinegar solution to remove the mold. Sterilize the board or mat with hot water and soap, and be sure you rinse the soap thoroughly.

CASE STUDY: DENA KING-NOSSOKOFF

Oakvale Farmstead Cheese
www.oakvalecheese.com

"We are fifth-generation dairy farmers who decided six years ago to use our knowledge and experience to produce a premium, wholesome cheese that we are proud of and distribute throughout the United States. Our family makes Farmstead Gouda, a cheese that originated in Holland. Holland's milk source is mainly Holstein-Friesian dairy cattle that produce higher fat and protein content than average U.S. Holsteins and less volume of milk.

"What I enjoy most about making cheese is the reaction from people when they bite into our Gouda. My favorite recipe for making cheese is the authentic Dutch recipe we use for our Farmstead Gouda. The most difficult thing about making cheese is matching the temperature of the milk to the culture being used during production."

CHAPTER 15

Mold- and Bacteria-Ripened Cheese

You began learning to make creamery products with the simple act of churning butter. As you churned, you watched cream transform into the wonderful and delicious solid that is an indispensable ingredient in so many recipes. You moved from making butter to inoculating dairy products with bacteria and enzymes to make cultured buttermilk, yogurt, and many soft, semi-soft, and hard cheeses. Now, you are at the pinnacle of cheese making as you move to the process of making mold- and bacteria-ripened cheese.

Making mold- and bacteria-ripened cheese is the most difficult, time-consuming, and particular skill in the practice. *You had a little experience in working with a mold- ripened cheese when you made chèvre in Chapter 11. You may want to review that recipe and the tips for inoculating the cheese as you begin this chapter.*

When you made chèvre, you inoculated that cheese with *Penicillium candidum*, a white mold that grows on the surface of the cheese. You will use that mold again in this chapter to make Brie. You will also use a blue mold called *Penicillium roqueforti* to make blue cheeses such as Stilton and Gorgonzola.

Brick Cheese

Brick is a bacteria-ripened cheese that is moderately difficult to make. Brick cheese is an American original that gets its name from the fact that it was first pressed between two bricks. Also, the cheese is shaped like a brick and should be no larger than a rectangular 10 by 5 by 3 inches. It is important that the cheese is not larger than that to accommodate bacterial growth and flavor development on the inside of the cheese. This recipe is a variation of Limburger cheese and has a flavor that ranges from moderately mild to very sharp and is influenced by the amount of time that the cheese is allowed to age.

Ingredients

2 gallons whole milk (cow's milk or goat's milk)

½ tsp powdered mesophilic starter (If you are using a prepared starter, use 4 ounces)

2 drops of liquid annatto cheese coloring diluted in ¼ cup of unchlorinated water (optional)

½ tablet vegetable rennet dissolved in ¼ cup of cool, unchlorinated water (Remember, if you are using powdered or rennet tablets, allow 20 to 30 minutes for the rennet to fully dissolve)

1 tsp *Brevibacterium linens* powder dissolved in 1 quart cool, unchlorinated water (red bacteria, also known as bacterial linens; this ingredient, like all other cheese-making ingredients and supplies, is available at cheese-making stores and online retailers. *You will find a list of these retailers in the resources section in the back of this book*)

2 pounds of cheese salt for brine solution

1 gallon cold water

Cheese wax

Directions

1. Pour the milk into a stainless-steel pot of a double boiler.

2. Bring the temperature of the milk to 85°.

3. Add the mesophilic starter and stir well with a whisk.

4. Remove the double boiler from the heat and allow the mixture 20 minutes to ripen.

5. If you are using the liquid annatto cheese coloring, add it now. Stir the mixture well to evenly distribute the coloring.

6. Add the diluted rennet mixture and stir gently for one minute.

7. Cover mixture and allow it to sit for 45 minutes to an hour.

8. At this point, the curds will be a thick, yogurt-like consistency.

9. Use a clean finger or a curd knife to check that the curds break cleanly when you cut them or insert your finger.

10. Cut the curds into ½-inch cubes.

11. Return the double boiler to the stove.

12. Slowly heat curds to 92°. Do this by increasing the temperature of the curds by 1° every five minutes. It should take you about 30 minutes to bring the curds to 92°.

13. Very gently stir as you heat the curds, allowing the curds to be evenly heated to prevent them from sticking together.

14. When the temperature of the curds reaches 92°, remove the double boiler from the stove.

15. Allow the curds to sit undisturbed for 15 minutes.

16. The curds should be at the bottom of the pot, covered by the liquid whey.

17. Fill a separate bowl or pot with about 1 gallon of 92° water. You will need the same amount of water as whey that you will remove from the pot of curds. You must also be sure that the water is the same temperature of the whey you will be removing from the pot.

18. Use a measuring cup to remove the whey that covers the curds. Keep track of the amount of whey you remove from the pot.

19. Remove the whey to the level of the curds.

20. Add the 92° water to the curds, adding exactly as much water as whey removed.

21. Gently stir the curds as you add the water.

22. Return the double boiler to the stove and maintain the temperature at 92° as you stir for 20 minutes.

23. After holding at 92° for 20 minutes, remove the double boiler from the stove and allow the curds to sit for 15 minutes.

24. Prepare a 2-pound cheese mold by lining it with cheesecloth. Place the cheese mold in a pan to catch the draining whey.

25. Use a slotted ladle to transfer the warm curds to a 2-pound cheese mold lined with cheesecloth.

26. Fold the cheesecloth over the top of the curd.

27. Place a follower on top of the wrapped curd and press the curd with 5 pounds of pressure for 15 minutes. The pressing should be done at room temperature.

28. Remove the cheese from the mold and unwrap it.

29. Turn the cheese over and rewrap it.

30. Place the rewrapped cheese back into the mold and press with 5 pounds of pressure for 15 minutes.

31. Repeat this process of pressing the cheese with 5 pounds of pressure for eight hours, turning the cheese every hour.

32. Prepare a saturated brine solution with 2 pounds of cheese salt and 1 gallon of cold water.

33. Soak the cheese in the brine solution for six hours. Flip the cheese three or four times during this period.

34. Remove the cheese from the brine solution and pat dry with a paper towel.

35. Set the cheese on a drying mat.

36. Pour 1 quart of cool, unchlorinated water into a sterilized spray bottle.

37. Add 1 tsp of *Brevibacterium linens* powder to the water in the spray bottle.

38. Shake the bottle well to ensure the powder is mixed well.

39. Spray all surfaces of the cheese with the mixture in the bottle.

40. Allow the cheese to sit uncovered on the cheese mat at 58° and 90 percent humidity for two weeks.

41. Wash the cheese by hand with a saline solution every day. Washing the cheese keeps the exterior of the cheese moist and encourages the growth of the *Brevibacterium linens.*

42. After about ten days, you will start to notice the growth of the red bacteria mold.

43. After two weeks, pat the surface of the cheese dry with a paper towel.

44. Wax the cheese as described in Chapter 10.

45. Allow the cheese to age at 45° to 50° for six to ten weeks.

Gorgonzola

Blue cheese is another example of a cheese that we often refer to as a specific kind of cheese, though it actually refers to an entire variety of cheese that includes Stilton, Roquefort, and Gorgonzola. The blue that is referenced when you think of these cheeses comes from the *Penicillium roqueforti* mold that is used to produce the blue veins and wonderful flavor we associate with blue cheese.

Making Gorgonzola is going to be a unique experience for those who are new to cheese making. You will be using a new ingredient (*Penicillium roqueforti*) and employing a new technique, as you will be combining two different batches of curds you will make over two days.

Gorgonzola is named after a village near Milan, Italy, where the cheese was developed. Gorgonzola has a wonderfully creamy, rich flavor with a crumbly texture. It is a great cheese to add to salads, as its flavor and texture complement the crispness and flavor of vegetables.

Ingredients

(This is the ingredient list for both batches. As you will be making two batches of curd, you will use half the amounts listed for each batch.)

2 gallons whole milk (cow's milk or goat's milk)

½ tsp powdered mesophilic starter (If you are using a prepared starter, use 4 ounces)

½ tablet vegetable rennet dissolved in ½ cup of cool, unchlorinated water (Remember, if you are using powdered or rennet tablets, allow 20 to 30 minutes for the rennet to fully dissolve. In this recipe, dilute ¼ tablet at a time in ½ cup of unchlorinated water)

¹/₈ tsp of rehydrated *Penicillium roqueforti* powder (You rehydrate the *Penicillium roqueforti* by sprinkling it on a ¼ cup of room-temperature milk. Allow the blue mold powder to sit on the milk for a minute before stirring it. Then, allow it to sit for 30 minutes before you add it to your recipe. Because you will be making two batches of curds with this recipe, you will rehydrate ¹/₁₆ tsp for each batch)

Cheese salt

Directions

1. Pour 1 gallon of milk into a stainless-steel pot of a double boiler or into a warm water bath.

2. Bring the temperature of the milk to 86°.

3. Add the first batch (half) of rehydrated *Penicillium roqueforti.*

4. Add half of the mesophilic starter and stir well with a whisk.

5. Cover the pot and allow the mixture 30 minutes to ripen.

6. Add half of the diluted rennet mixture and stir gently for one minute.

7. Cover mixture and allow it to sit at 86° for 45 minutes to an hour.

8. At this point, the curds will be a thick, yogurt-like consistency.

9. Use a clean finger or a curd knife to check that the curds break cleanly when you cut them or insert your finger.

10. Cut the curds into ½-inch cubes.

11. Allow the cut curds to sit for 10 minutes.

12. Line a colander with a large, doubled piece of cheesecloth. Make sure the cloth is large enough that you will be able to bring the corners together in a bag for the cheese to drain. Place the colander over a pot to catch the whey.

13. Gently pour the curds into the cheesecloth-lined colander.

14. Allow curds to drain in colander for about ten minutes.

15. Bring and tie corners of cheesecloth together to form a bag.

16. Hang the bag over the pot, allowing it to drain at room temperature overnight.

The next morning, repeat the process to this point using the second half of the ingredients. When you are at this point, you will have two batches of curds. The second batch of curd should be allowed to drain for one hour prior to continuing with the recipe.

17. Remove the first batch of curds (from the previous night) from the bag and place on a sterilized cutting board.

18. Cut the first batch of curds into 1-inch cubes.

19. Place the cubed curds into a large mixing bowl.

20. Remove the second batch of curds from the bag and place on a sterilized cutting board.

21. Cut the second batch of curds into 1-inch cubes.

22. Place the cubed curds into a separate mixing bowl.

23. Gently mix 2 tbsp of salt into each bowl of curds.

24. Sterilize your 2-pound cheese mold, two cheese mats, and two cheese boards.

25. Place a cheese mat on a cheese board and then place the cheese mold on the cheese mat.

26. Spoon half or the second batch of curds into the bottom and around the sides of the cheese mold. You want to make a cavity in the center of the curds.

27. Spoon all of the first batch of curds into the cavity created by the second batch.

28. Spoon the remainder of the second batch of curds over the top of everything in the mold.

29. Place another cheese mat on top of the mold and a cheese board on top of the mat.

30. You now have a stack: board/mat/mold with curd/mat/board.

31. Allow this stack to sit at a temperature of 60° for two hours.

32. Flip the stack every 15 minutes during these two hours.

33. Over the next three days, flip the stack several times a day.

34. After three days, remove the cheese from the mold.

35. Sprinkle salt over the entire outer surface of the cheese, then shake off any loose salt.

36. Allow the cheese to age for four days at a temperature of 55° and a relative humidity of 85 percent.

37. Lightly rub salt of the cheese each day over this four-day aging.

38. After four days, use a sterilized pick, skewer, or knitting needle (about $\frac{1}{16}$-inch diameter) to poke 25 holes through the cheese from the top to the bottom. The holes allow air to get into the cheese to facilitate the growth of the bacteria.

39. Age the cheese for 30 days at a temperature of 55°.

40. After 30 days, age the cheese at 50° and a relative humidity of 85 percent for three months.

41. During this three-month period, wipe or scrape the cheese clean of all exterior mold with a knife.

42. After three months, your cheese is ready to be eaten, though you can age it as long as six months.

Stilton

Another blue cheese that is only moderately difficult to make but wonderful to eat is Stilton. Stilton is a traditionally English cheese and is, in fact, the only name-protected cheese made in England, meaning it cannot be commercially manufactured elsewhere and sold as Stilton cheese. In protecting the name of Stilton cheese, the British High Court defined the cheese as a blue or white cheese made from full-cream cow's milk with no applied pressure that could be pierced but not inoculated; that forms its own crust or coat; and that is made in a cylindrical form, the milk coming from English dairy herds in the district of Melton Mowbray and the surrounding areas falling within the counties of Leicestershire, Derbyshire, and Nottinghamshire.

The recipe below cannot, by strict definition, be called Stilton because you will probably not be making it from the milk that comes from English dairy herds in the district of Melton Mowbray. However, the recipes given below describe the methods you can employ to make excellent replicas of both blue and white Stilton-like cheeses.

Stilton Blue

Ingredients
2 gallons whole cow's milk

2 cups cream (heavy, light, or half and half is acceptable)

⅛ tsp of rehydrated *Penicillium roqueforti* powder (You rehydrate the *Penicillium roqueforti* by sprinkling it on a ¼ cup of room-temperature milk. Allow the blue mold powder to sit on the milk for a minute before stirring it. Then, allow it to sit for 30 minutes before you add it to your recipe)

½ tsp powdered mesophilic starter (If you are using a prepared starter, use 4 ounces)

¼ tablet vegetable rennet dissolved in ¼ cup of cool, unchlorinated water (Remember, if you are using powdered or rennet tablets, allow 20 to 30 minutes for the rennet to fully dissolve. In this recipe, dilute ¼ tablet at a time in ¼ cup of unchlorinated water)

2 tbsp cheese salt

Directions

1. Pour the milk and cream into a stainless-steel pot of a double boiler or into a warm water bath.

2. Bring the temperature of the milk/cream to 86°.

3. Add the rehydrated *Penicillium roqueforti* and stir well.

4. Add the mesophilic starter and stir well with a whisk.

5. Cover the pot and allow the mixture 30 minutes to ripen at 86°.

6. Add the diluted rennet mixture and stir gently for one minute.

7. Cover mixture and allow it to sit at 86° for an hour to 90 minutes.

8. At this point, the curds will be a thick, yogurt-like consistency.

9. Use a clean finger or a curd knife to check that the curds break cleanly when you cut them or insert your finger.

10. Cut the curds into ½-inch cubes.

11. Allow the cut curds to sit for 20 minutes.

12. Line a colander with a large, doubled piece of cheesecloth. Make sure the cloth is large enough that you will be able to bring the corners together in a bag for the cheese to drain. Place the colander in a pot to catch the whey. The colander should be able to sit in the pot so the curds will rest in the whey after they are transferred to the colander. The pot should be in a warm water bath so you will be able to hold the temperature of the whey at 86°.

13. Use a slotted spoon or ladle to gently transfer the curds into the cheese-cloth-lined colander. The curds should be in the colander, resting in the whey.

14. Allow the curds to sit in the whey at 86° for 90 minutes.

15. Bring the corners of the cheesecloth together to form a bag, and hang the bag of curds over the pot to drain.

16. Allow curds to drain for about 30 minutes.

17. After the curds have stopped dripping, place the bag of curds on a sterilized cutting board (the curds remain in the bag) and place another sterilized cutting board or plate on top of the bag. This should be done in a place where the curds can continue to drain.

18. Place a 5-pound weight on the plate/top cutting board.

19. Press the curds in this manner at room temperature for 12 hours.

20. Remove the curds from the bag and transfer them to a bowl.

21. Break the curds up into 1-inch pieces with clean fingers, being careful not to work the curds too hard.

22. Gently add the salt by hand.

23. Sterilize a 2-pound cheese mold, two cheese mats, and two cheese boards.

24. Place a cheese mat on a cheese board, then place the cheese mold on the cheese mat.

25. Spoon the curds into the cheese mold.

26. Place another cheese mat on top of the mold and a cheese board on top of the mat.

27. You now have a stack: board/mat/mold with curd/mat/board.

28. Allow this stack to sit at a temperature of 70° for two hours. Room temperature will do for this two-hour period.

29. Flip the stack every 15 minutes during these two hours.

30. Allow the cheese to rest for 12 hours at room temperature.

31. Over the next four days, flip the stack four times a day.

32. After four days, remove the cheese from the mold.

33. Use a sterilized pick, skewer, or knitting needle (about 1/16-inch diameter) to poke 25 holes through the cheese from the top to the bottom. The holes allow air to get into the cheese to facilitate the growth of the bacteria.

34. Age the cheese for 90 days at a temperature of 50° and a relative humidity of 85 percent.

35. During this three-month period, wipe or scrape the cheese clean of all exterior mold with a knife.

36. After three months, your cheese is ready to be tasted, though you can age it as long as six months.

Stilton White

There are several slight variations to the above recipe that will make a white cheese with a milder flavor that is comparable to a medium-sharp cheddar . This is a wonderful dessert cheese that can be made with fruit incorporated into it, much the same way that herbs and spices are incorporated into other cheeses such as cheddar or Gouda. Directions for incorporating fruit follow the recipe below:

Ingredients

2 gallons whole cow's milk

2 cups cream (heavy, light, or half and half is acceptable)

½ tsp powdered mesophilic starter (If you are using a prepared starter, use 4 ounces)

¼ tablet vegetable rennet dissolved in ¼ cup of cool, unchlorinated water (Remember, if you are using powdered or rennet tablets, allow 20 to 30 minutes for the rennet to fully dissolve. In this recipe, dilute ¼ tablet at a time in ¼ cup of unchlorinated water)

2 tbsp cheese salt

Directions

1. Pour the milk and cream into a stainless-steel pot of a double boiler or into a warm water bath.

2. Bring the temperature of the milk/cream to 86°.

3. Add the mesophilic starter and stir well with a whisk.

4. Cover the pot and allow the mixture 30 minutes to ripen at 86°.

5. Add the diluted rennet mixture and stir gently for one minute.

6. Cover mixture and allow it to sit at 86° for an hour to 90 minutes.

7. At this point, the curds will be a thick, yogurt-like consistency.

8. Use a clean finger or a curd knife to check that the curds break cleanly when you cut them or insert your finger.

9. Cut the curds into ½-inch cubes.

10. Allow the cut curds to sit for 20 minutes.

11. Line a colander with a large, doubled piece of cheesecloth. Make sure the cloth is large enough that you will be able to bring the corners together in a bag for the cheese to drain. Place the colander in a pot to catch the whey. The colander should be able to sit in the pot so the curds will rest in the whey after they are transferred to the colander. The pot should be in a warm water bath so you will be able to hold the temperature of the whey at 86°.

12. Use a slotted spoon or ladle to gently transfer the curds into the cheese-cloth-lined colander. The curds should be in the colander resting in the whey.

13. Allow the curds to sit in the whey at the target temperature for 90 minutes.

14. Bring the corners of the cheesecloth together to form a bag and hang the bag of curds over the pot to drain.

15. Allow curds to drain for about 30 minutes.

16. After the curds have stopped dripping, place the bag of curds on a sterilized cutting board (the curds remain in the bag) and place another sterilized cutting board or plate on top of the bag. This should be done in a place where the curds can continue to drain.

17. Place a 5-pound weight on the plate/top cutting board.

18. Press the curds in this manner at room temperature for 12 hours.

19. Remove the curds from the bag and transfer them to a bowl.

20. Break the curds up into 1-inch pieces with clean fingers, being careful not to work the curds too hard.

21. Gently add the salt by hand.

22. Sterilize a 2-pound cheese mold, two cheese mats, and two cheese boards.

23. Place a cheese mat on a cheese board, then place the cheese mold on the cheese mat.

24. Spoon the curds into the cheese mold.

25. Place another cheese mat on top of the mold and a cheese board on top of the mat.

26. You now have a stack: board/mat/mold with curd/mat/board.

27. Allow this stack to sit at a temperature of 70° for two hours. Room temperature will do for this two-hour period.

28. Flip the stack every 15 minutes during these two hours.

29. Allow the cheese to rest for 12 hours at room temperature.

30. After a day or two, the cheese should be firm enough to remove from the mold.

31. Allow the cheese to air dry at room temperature.

32. After the cheese feels dry to the touch, age the cheese for four days at a temperature of 50° and a relative humidity of 85 percent. Turn the cheese four times a day during this four-day period.

33. Age the cheese for four months at 50° and a relative humidity of 85 percent. During this four-month period, wipe the cheese off with a paper towel dampened in a brine solution once a week.

34. After four months, your cheese is ready to be tasted, though you can age it as long as six months.

Adding fruit to your Stilton White

You can add dried blueberries, cherries, cranberries, candied ginger, or just about any dried fruit to the above recipe by following these simple directions:

Ingredients
1 to 2 tbsp dried fruit (finely chopped ginger, dates, or any sweet fruit that you prefer is acceptable)

¼ cup water

Directions
1. Place the fruit in a vegetable steamer.

2. Steam fruit for 15 minutes.

3. Add ¼ cup of water the fruit was steamed in to milk/cream mixture prior to adding starter culture.

4. Add steamed fruit to curds when you add the salt before you place curds in cheese mold.

5. Proceed with Stilton White recipe as described.

Perhaps the most difficult aspect of making bacteria- and mold-ripened cheese is having the patience to wait three to six months to enjoy the fruits of your labor. You are advised to be patient on numerous occasions throughout this book. Patience really pays off when you get into making these complex recipes.

From soft cheese to semi-soft, from Italian cheese to mold- and bacteria-ripened cheese, you have now employed nearly every cheese-making technique in the book. There are, of course, many other cheese recipes that have not been covered here, but you are sure discover them as you continue to experiment and create a wide variety of cheeses now that you have the know-how and experience.

Troubleshooting Mold- and Bacteria-Ripened Cheese

If your has a sponge-like appearance when you cut into it after aging:

*   An unwanted bacterium has probably contaminated your cheese. Next time, pay closer attention to cleanliness and sterilization procedures before and during the cheese-making process.

If the surface of your aging cheese develops rampant mold growth:

*   You may have the problem of ambient mold growth in the place you are aging your cheese. Cleanliness of the aging facility is just as important as cleanliness of your utensils. Another problem may be lack of good ventilation in your aging facility. Be sure that air is moving around properly in the place you store and age your cheese.

CASE STUDY: LINDA DIMMICK

Neighborly Farms of Vermont
www.neighborlyfarms.com

Linda Dimmick and her husband began to transition their dairy farm to an organic farm in the late 1990s. They began manufacturing cheese commercially from their farm in April 2001, and it took them a full year to build a cheese manufacturing room on their farm.

"It is very satisfying work to produce 900 pounds of cheese in one day," Dimmick said. "It is also exciting to have your name on a product that people enjoy. We have a very faithful following. Going into the cheese room for the day is sort of an escape for me. I don't take any phone calls and just focus on what needs to be done. It is not rushed; it just happens in its own time."

Dimmick said the hardest thing for her has been the physical toll cheese making has taken on her body. She said the 40-pound box mold will weigh up to 65 pounds once it is filled with curds.

"I developed muscles I didn't even know I had," she said.

The Dimmicks make cheddar, Colby, Monterey Jack, and feta on their farm using standardized recipes. She said Monterey Jack and Colby cheeses are easier to make because they do not go through the cheddaring process. Dimmick said she was a little naïve when she first started making cheese because she thought if you bought cheese-making equipment, the cheese would essentially make itself.

"I really didn't realize how physical the work was," she said. "Another thing to consider is just because you have the cheese in your cooler, doesn't mean it will sell. I have done a lot of marketing over the years, and it doesn't let up; you have to keep doing it to continue your success."

CHAPTER 16

Great Recipes with Cheese, Butter, and Yogurt

Whey-Out Whole-Wheat Bread

Though this recipe calls for liquid whey, you can substitute the same amount of homemade cultured buttermilk. This recipe was a ribbon winner at the 2009 Nebraska State Fair. If you use buttermilk, you can omit the ⅔ cup of dry milk.

Ingredients
1 package yeast
2 ½ cups warm liquid whey (about 105°)*
⅔ cup dry milk
½ cup honey
2 tsp coarse kosher salt
4 tbsp melted butter
4 cups (approximately) white unbleached flour
3 ½ cups (approximately) whole-wheat flour
*The ribbon-winning recipe used whey from cow's milk and separated from the curds while making cottage cheese. You can also use whey collected from yogurt.

Directions

1. In a large mixing bowl, proof yeast in warm whey.

2. Whisk in dry milk, honey, salt, and melted butter.

3. Whisk in, 1 cup at a time, 3 cups of white unbleached flour.

4. By this time the dough should be starting to get fairly stiff.

5. Using the dough hooks of an electric mixer, mix in the whole-wheat flour about ¼ cup at a time until the dough starts to come away from the sides of the bowl.

6. Using a large spoon or spatula, mix in white unbleached flour until the dough starts to lose some of its stickiness.

7. Turn the dough out onto a floured surface and knead until the dough is soft, smooth, and not sticky.

8. Put the dough in a large buttered bowl, cover, and let rise in a warm place until doubled in size (about an hour).

9. After the dough has risen, punch it down and turn it out onto a floured surface.

10. Cut the dough in half and shape into two loaves.

11. Place loaves into buttered 8.5- by 4.5- by 2.5-inch loaf pans.

12. Cover loaves with a light towel and let rise until they are about 1 inch over the top of the pans.

13. Bake in a preheated oven at 375° for about 45 minutes. Cover loosely with foil after about 25 minutes to keep the tops from getting too brown.

14. Remove from pans and cool on racks immediately upon removing from oven.

15. Cool completely before putting into plastic bags.

Absolutely the Best Macaroni and Cheese

Make this mac and cheese for your family once and you will be asked to make it over and over again. Do not let the word macaroni fool you; you can use any kind of pasta that your heart (or your kids) desire. The recipe calls for cheddar cheese, but you may substitute any good melting cheese you wish. Muenster or Swiss cheese would also be very good in this recipe.

Ingredients

1 pound pasta (small pasta, such as elbow, shells, or farfalle work better than pasta like spaghetti or linguine)

3 tbsp homemade butter

⅔ cup of milk (whole, low-fat, or skim)

2 tbsp white flour

1 tsp dry mustard

2 tbsp plus 1 tsp salt

2 cups finely grated cheddar cheese (more or less to taste)

Directions

1. Prepare a 2-quart glass baking dish by covering the inside surface with 1 tbsp of the butter.

2. Preheat oven to 375°.

3. Fill a large pot with water and add 2 tbsp salt. The pot needs to be big enough so the pasta has a lot of room to cook. If the pot is overly full of pasta, the pasta will cook to be sticky.

4. Bring water to a full boil.

5. Add pasta to boiling water and stir it constantly for about a minute.

6. Cook pasta to al dente (slightly firm and not overcooked). The cooking time of the pasta will vary depending of the type of pasta you choose and the brand. If the pasta has a suggested cooking time on its packaging, test the pasta a minute before it is supposed to be done. To test the pasta,

retrieve one or two pieces of pasta from the pot with a slotted spoon. Blow on the pasta for a few seconds to cool it off and taste it. It should be cooked but firm — not mushy.

7. When the pasta is cooked, very carefully pour the pasta into a colander in the sink to drain.

8. Rinse the cooked pasta with cold water to stop the cooking process. If the pasta seems a little undercooked, that is all right. You are going to bake the pasta and it will soften up as it bakes.

9. Allow the pasta to drain.

10. In a heavy-bottom saucepan, melt 2 tbsp of your homemade butter over a medium-low heat.

11. Use a whisk to mix the flour, salt, and dry mustard into the butter. The mixture will be paste-like.

12. With the stove still at medium low, whisk the milk into the butter about ½ cup at a time.

13. Increase the heat to medium-high and stir constantly until the milk mixture starts to bubble.

14. As soon as the mixture starts to bubble, remove it from the heat.

15. Whisk in 1 ½ cups of the cheese. The cheese will melt into the hot milk mixture.

16. Stir the pasta into the milk/cheese mixture with a large spoon.

17. Pour the pasta/cheese mixture into the butter-prepared baking dish.

18. Cover the top of the pasta mixture with the rest of the grated cheese.

19. Bake for 25 minutes or until the cheese on top of the dish just starts to brown.

20. Remove from oven and allow to sit for ten minutes.

Impossible Quiche

This recipe is from Emily Montgomery at Calkin's Creamery.

Ingredients
12 slices bacon, fried and crumbled

1 cup grated Gouda cheese

¼ cup chopped onion

2 cups milk

5 eggs

½ cup Bisquick®

Salt and pepper to taste

Directions
1. Heat oven to 350°.

2. Lightly grease 10-inch pie plate.

3. Sprinkle bacon, onion, and cheese in plate.

4. Blend remaining ingredients at high speed for one minute.

5. Spread blended ingredients over bacon, onion, and cheese.

6. Bake until golden brown (about 50 minutes).

7. Let stand 15 minutes before cutting.

8. Can be reheated, if necessary.

Pretty Perfect Pizza

After your family and friends taste your Pretty Perfect Pizza, they might suggest that you open your own pizza parlor. Cooking for family and friends is a passionate act of love, and making a great homemade pizza expresses that love more than just about any other food, especially when that pizza is made using your own homemade buttermilk and cheese.

Making your own pizza is a wonderful way to please every taste in your circle because everyone loves pizza. You can either make individual pizzas or a large pizza with different toppings on different parts of the pie.

Offered here is a basic crust recipe that is followed by suggestions and recipes for several great toppings. Pizza is a dish that calls for a great amount of creativity. The toppings are only suggestions, but there is a great pesto recipe among them.

The crust

Ingredients

1 cup warm whey or homemade cultured buttermilk (The whey or buttermilk should be about 90° to 100°)

1 package active dry yeast proofed in ½ cup of 90° to 100° water (To proof the yeast, pour the warm water in a large mixing bowl and pour the yeast into the water. Allow the yeast to sit undisturbed for about 5 minutes. At this point, you will start to see the yeast "explode" in the water. You will notice movement that tells you that the yeast is active)

1 tsp salt

2 tbsp olive oil

Approximately 4 cups of unbleached white flour

Directions

1. Add the whey/buttermilk to the bowl the yeast has been proofing in and mix well with a whisk.

2. Add salt and whisk well.

3. Add olive oil and whisk well.

4. Add flour ½ cup at a time, whisking and mixing well with each addition.

5. The more flour you add, the thicker and stickier the dough will become.

6. As the dough becomes too thick to mix with the whisk, use a large wooden spoon to incorporate the flour.

7. Add flour until the dough starts to come away from the side of the bowl.

8. Spread flour on a flat work surface counter or table.

9. Transfer the sticky dough to the floured work surface.

10. Knead the dough by hand just until you can hold it in your hand for five seconds without having the dough stick to your hands.

11. Prepare a separate bowl by covering the interior surface of the bowl with a coat of olive oil.

12. Place the dough in the prepared bowl and turn it over once. Turning the dough over gives the top of the dough a thin coat of olive oil and prevents it from becoming dry as the dough rises.

13. Cover the bowl with a lid or dishcloth and allow the dough to rise in a warm place for an hour or until the dough has doubled in size.

14. After the dough has risen, punch it down in the bowl and turn it back out onto your work surface.

15. Knead the dough for a minute.

16. Return the dough to the bowl it rose in and cover it.

17. Place the bowl of dough in the refrigerator and allow it to cool for several hours.

18. Check the dough after 90 minutes. If it has risen to the top of the bowl, punch it down again and return it to the refrigerator.

Pesto Pizza

You can put anything on top of a pizza. If you travel a good deal, it is always an interesting experience to order a local pizza. You probably know the difference between the thin-crust New York pizza and thick-crust Chicago pizza. Order a pizza in London and you may be offered fried eggs as a topper; order a pizza in Moscow and you may get one topped with pot cheese, potatoes, and apples.

Ingredients

1 batch pizza dough
2 cups fresh basil leaves
¼ cup pine nuts
2 cloves garlic, pressed
¼ cup olive oil
3 tbsp finely grated homemade Parmesan cheese
1 cup grated homemade Mozzarella cheese
Corn meal (enough to lightly dust the pizza pan)
Salt to taste

Directions

1. Prepare the dough for the crust as described above.

2. Preheat oven to 400°.

3. Put basil, pine nuts, pressed garlic, and olive oil into a food processor and process until like a paste.

4. Mix Parmesan cheese into basil mixture by hand.

5. Roll pizza dough out into shape and thickness desired.

6. Prepare a pizza pan or sheet by brushing a thin coat of olive oil on it and lightly dusting it with corn meal.

7. Place rolled and shaped dough onto prepared pizza pan.

8. Lightly brush surface of dough with olive oil.

9. Lightly salt surface of dough.

10. Spread a thin layer of pesto over the surface of the pizza.

11. Cover pesto with Mozzarella.

12. Bake 15 minutes or until Mozzarella begins to brown.

13. If you like a thicker-crust pizza, you might bake the crust for about 5 minutes after you lightly salt it and prior to adding the pesto to the dough.

Old Windmill Dairy Lime and de Coconut

This comes from the Lobaughs at The Old Windmill Dairy who say, "If you like dessert, this recipe will knock your socks off."

Ingredients

3 5-ounce containers of Old Windmill Dairy Lime and de Coconut

1 pint of heavy whipping cream

½ cup sugar

2 tbsp of key lime juice

1 9-inch graham cracker crust.

Directions

1. Whip heavy cream until it forms peaks.

2. Mix sugar and key lime juice together well.

3. Fold the Lime and de Coconut, whipping cream, and sugar and key lime mixture together.

4. Spread into graham cracker crust.

5. For extra flavoring, try serving with coconut shavings or shaved chocolate.

6. Refrigerate for an hour before serving.

Double Key-Lime Cheesecake

Ingredients

1 cup graham cracker crumbs

4 tbsp softened homemade butter

8 to 12 key limes

1 ¼ cup(s) sugar

¼ cup cornstarch

½ cup softened homemade cream cheese

1 cup homemade ricotta cheese (a simple pot cheese will work, too)

4 large eggs

2 cups of light cream

2 tsp vanilla extract

Prepare the ricotta cheese using the following recipe:

Ingredients
1 gallon whole milk

⅓ cup key lime juice (this is the amount of juice in about ¾ pound or four to five key limes)

Salt (to taste)

Directions
1. Pour milk into a large, heavy-bottom, stainless-steel pot.

2. Slowly heat directly on stovetop to 180° to 185°.

3. Stir occasionally. You do not want the milk to scorch, but too much stirring will result in curds that are too small.

4. Stir lime juice into milk.

5. Put the milk back on the heat and stir for about 30 seconds.

6. Remove milk from heat and continue to stir until curds form.

7. Allow milk to sit for 30 minutes. Do not stir during at this time.

8. Line a colander with a large, doubled piece of cheesecloth. Make sure the cloth is large enough that you will be able to bring the corners together in a bag for the cheese to drain. Place the colander over a pot to catch the whey.

9. Gently pour the curds into the cheesecloth-lined colander.

10. Make a bag by tying the corners of the cheesecloth together.

11. Hang the bag of curds over the pot and allow them to drain for an hour.

12. Remove the curds from the bag and place them in a bowl.

13. Salt to taste.

14. Set ricotta aside.

For pie:

15. Preheat oven to 375°.

16. Wrap outside of 9-inch springform pan with heavy-duty foil to prevent batter from leaking out during baking.

17. In a separate bowl, mix graham cracker crumbs and butter with a fork until crumbs are completely and evenly moistened.

18. Press crumb mixture firmly onto bottom of pan with fingers.

19. Bake crust ten minutes.

20. Cool crust in pan on wire rack for about 15 minutes.

21. Reset oven to 325°.

22. From four key limes, grate 4 tsp peel and squeeze ⅓ cup juice.

23. Stir together sugar and cornstarch in small bowl until well-blended.

24. Beat cream cheese and ricotta until smooth in a large mixing bowl. Use a mixer on medium speed for about five minutes.

25. Slowly beat sugar mixture into cheese mixture.

26. Reduce mixer speed to low and beat in eggs one at a time.

27. Beat in cream, vanilla, lime peel, and juice until just blended. Scrape bowl frequently with rubber spatula.

28. Pour batter onto crust.

29. Bake cheesecake one hour.

30. Turn off oven and allow cheesecake to remain in oven for one hour.

31. Remove cheesecake from oven.

32. Run a knife between the edge of your cheesecake and the pan as soon as the cheesecake comes out of oven to prevent cracking during cooling.

33. Cool cake in pan on wire rack three hours.

34. Cover and refrigerate cheesecake overnight.

35. Remove side of pan and foil and place cake on plate to serve.

Amaltheia Ricotta Goat Cheese Cups

This recipe is courtesy of Susan Brown at Amaltheia Organic Dairy.

"A favorite recipe that I would like to share is for a sweet cheese made with our ricotta goat cheese. It is beautiful and delicious," she said.

Ingredients
Amaltheia ricotta goat cheese
Honey (to taste)
Filo dough cups
Berries

Directions
1. Allow ricotta to soften.
2. Add honey to taste.
3. Fill filo dough cups with ricotta/honey mix.
4. Top with a berry (blackberry, blueberry, raspberry).

CONCLUSION

It is quite amazing the number of things that can be done with a gallon of milk and a few ingredients. As you review the recipes for all the creamery items noted in this book, you might be surprised at the similarities in the recipes, yet the great variety of outcomes.

The common advice issued by most of the Case Study participants is that the best way to learn how to make cheese, butter, and yogurt is to just do it — and then do it again. Keep trying until you get it right. There is no substitute for experience. Do not let the frustration of a grainy Mozzarella get you down. Feed it to the chickens or the kids and try it again.

If you have the opportunity to visit a small artisan cheese maker, make the time and do it. You will learn a good deal by seeing it done and talking to people who make cheese on a daily basis. The people who make cheese are passionate about doing so, and most are quite eager to talk about it.

Aside from the advice of persistence, also heed the many warnings about cleanliness because it is of vital importance. Go the extra mile to make sure that all of your working surfaces and utensils are sterile prior to starting. These preparations will save your cheese as well as the health of those who enjoy your lovingly made products.

As you ensure the cleanliness of your kitchen, also make sure that you work with the freshest of products. Read labels and expiration dates. Learn as much as you can about where your ingredients come from.

Get to know a dairy farmer. If you live in an area where you have access to farm-fresh milk, give it a try. There is a lot to be said for community-supported agriculture. *Check out the resource section of this book to guide you to places where you can get farm-fresh milk in your area.*

Finally, share your homemade cheese, butter, and yogurt. It is always a wonderful gift.

RESOURCES

Supplies for making cheese and other creamery products

New England Cheese Making Supply Company
www.cheesemaking.com
PO Box 85
Ashfield, MA 01330
413-628-3808

Dairy Connection, Inc.
www.dairyconnection.com
501 Tasman St.
Suite B
Madison, WI 53714
Contact: Jeff Meier or Cathy Potter
E-mail: getculture@ameritech.net
Phone: 608-242-9030
Fax: 608-242-9036

Glengarry Cheesemaking and Dairy Supply

www.glengarrycheesemaking.on.ca

PO Box 92

Massena, NY, 13662

Or

PO Box 190

#5926 County Road 34

Lancaster, Ontario. K0C 1N0, Canada

Phone: 1-888-816-0903 or (613) 347-1141

Fax: (613) 347-1167

info@glengarrycheesemaking.on.ca or glengarrycheesemaking@bellnet.ca

Where Can I Find Real Milk?

www.realmilk.com/where2.html

About cheese, butter, and yogurt

All About Cheese

www.cheese.com

American Cheese Society

www.cheesesociety.org

Directory of U.S. Cheese Makers

www.forkandbottle.com/cheese/uscheese.htm

The Cheese Ambassador

www.thecheeseambassador.com

National Yogurt Association

http://aboutyogurt.com

GLOSSARY OF TERMS

Acidity – This refers to the percentage of lactic acid in dairy products. High levels of acidity are created by introducing a starter culture or by adding various types of acid, such as vinegar or citric acid.

Aging – Storing cheese for extended periods of time, allowing it to develop enhanced flavor and texture.

Annatto – An orange coloring agent from the seeds of a South American shrub called achiote.

Brevibacterium linens – A red bacteria that is usually applied to the exterior of cheese with washed rinds.

Bacteria – Single-celled microorganisms that are present everywhere. Lactic acid-producing bacteria are introduced to dairy products in a controlled manner to produce various cheese products.

Bath – Warm or cold water used to heat milk or wash curds while making milk and other creamery items.

Brining – Washing or soaking cheese in water saturated with salt.

Calcium chloride – A form of powdered salt. Calcium chloride is an optional ingredient in cheese making but is quite beneficial to settle the curd.

Casein – A type of milk protein.

Cheddaring – The process of slicing cheese-curd mass; used to make cheddar cheese.

Cheese molds – Baskets used to shape and drain cheese curd.

Cheese press – A mechanical device used to force whey from cheese curd and shape cheese in a cheese mold.

Cheese wax – A very supple wax with a low melting point; used to protect cheese during the aging process.

Coagulation – When casein in milk clots and sets as the curd forms.

Curd – Solid mass formed by heating coagulated milk.

Curd knife – A long-handled, flat-bladed utensil used to cut cheese curd.

Direct-set cultures – Prepackaged, single-use dried starter added directly to milk; used to encourage lactic acid production.

Drying – Air-drying of cheese to help form a protective rind for the aging process.

Geotrichum candidum – A white surface mold that is used in making soft cheese such as Brie or Camembert.

Grating cheese – Cheese, such as Parmesan or Romano, with a texture that allows it to be grated.

Homogenization – The process of heating milk to break down the fat globules, rendering a uniformity to the liquid.

Lactic acid – The acid created in milk by starter cultures introduced during the cheese-making process.

Lactose – A naturally occurring sugar found in milk.

Milling – Breaking the curd up into uniform size and shape.

Mesophilic starter – Lactic acid-producing bacteria used to make cheese when the milk is heated below 102°.

Pasteurization – The process of heating milk to high temperatures to destroy harmful pathogenic organisms.

Penicillium candidum – White surface mold used to ripen soft cheeses such as Brie and Camembert.

Penicillium roqueforti – Blue mold used in and on the surface of blue cheeses such as Gorgonzola and Stilton.

Pressing – The application of pressure on curds to expel excess whey and help shape them.

Propionic shermanii – An enzyme used to produce holes in Swiss-type cheese.

Rennet – An enzyme produced in the fourth stomach of a calk and in various plants that is used to coagulate milk to make cheese.

Ripening – The increasing of lactic acid and milk sugars in milk from the introduction of a starter culture.

Starter culture – Bacteria prepared to be introduced to milk to assist in the production of lactic acid and milk sugar.

Thermophilic starter – Lactic acid-producing bacteria used to make cheese when the milk is heated above 102°.

Washed curds – A process of replacing whey with water after the separation of the curds and whey.

Whey – The liquid that develops after the milk coagulates and begins to curdle. Whey contains water, lactose, minerals, and proteins.

BIBLIOGRAPHY

Biss, Kathy, *Practical Cheesemaking*, Wiltshire, England, Crowood Press, 1988.

Carroll, Ricki, *Home Cheese Making*, North Adams, MA, Storey Publishing, 2002.

Ciletti, Barbara, *Making Great Cheese at Home*, New York, N.Y., Lark Books, 1999.

Farrell-Kingsley, Kathy, *The Home Creamery*, North Adams, MA, Storey Publishing, 2008.

Jenkins, Steve, *Cheese Primer*, New York, N.Y., Workman Publishing, 1996.

Smith, Tim, *Making Artisan Cheese*, Beverly, MA, Quarry Books, 2005.

Sokol, Shane, *And That's How You Make Cheese!*, Lincoln, NE, Writer's Club Press, 2001.

AUTHOR BIOGRAPHY

Richard Helweg has more than 25 years' experience working in the non-profit sector as an artistic director, managing director, and executive director. He is an award-winning playwright and has recently written *...And Justice for All, A History of the Supreme Court*, a book for young readers, and *How to Get Your Share of the $30-Plus Billion Being Offered by U.S. Foundations: A Complete Guide for Locating, Preparing, and Presenting Your Proposals* (Atlantic Publishing). Richard lives in Lincoln, Nebraska, with his wife, Karen, and sons Aedan and Rory.

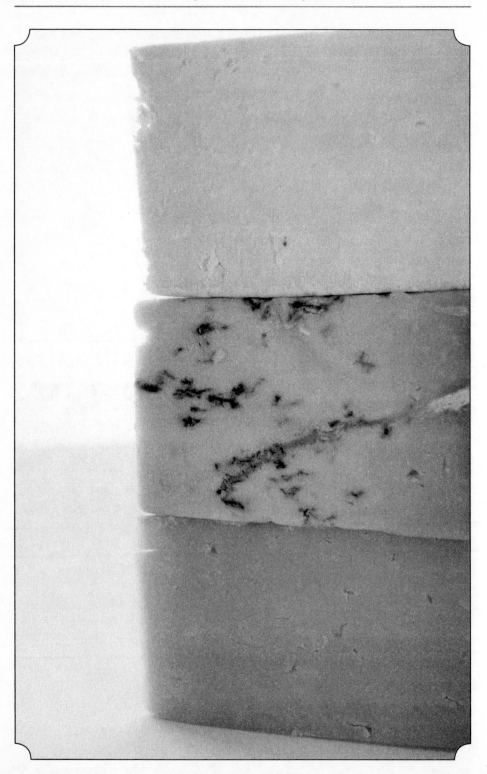

INDEX